Japan Business and Economics Series

This series provides a forum for empirical and theoretical work on Japanese business enterprise, Japanese management practices, and the Japanese economy. Japan continues to grow as a major economic world power, and Japanese companies create products and deliver services that compete successfully with those of the best firms around the world. Much can be learned from an understanding of how this has been accomplished and how it is being sustained.

The series aims to balance empirical and theoretical work, always in search of a deeper understanding of the Japanese phenomenon. It also implicitly takes for granted that there are significant differences between Japan and other countries and that these differences are worth knowing about. The series editors expect books published in the series to present a broad range of work on social, cultural, economic, and political institutions. If, as some have predicted, the twenty-first century sees the rise of Asia as the largest economic region in the world, the rest of the world needs to understand the country that is, and will continue to be, one of the major players in this region.

Editorial Board

Japan Business and Economics Series

Knowledge-Driven Work

. . . .

Unexpected Lessons from Japanese and United States Work Practices

Joel Cutcher-Gershenfeld   Wen-Jeng Lin
Michio Nitta   Michael Moore
Betty J. Barrett   William M. Mothersell
Nejib Belhedi   Jennifer Palthe
Simon Sai-Chung Chow   Shobha Ramanand
Takashi Inaba   Mark E. Strolle
Iwao Ishino   Arthur C. Wheaton

*With additional contributions by the following
members of the Work Practices Diffusion Team:*

Cheryl Coutchie, Seepa Lee, and Stacia Rabine

Foreword by Thomas A. Kochan and Haruo Shimada

New York • Oxford • Oxford University Press 1998

Oxford University Press

Oxford   New York
Athens   Auckland   Bangkok   Bogotá   Buenos Aires   Calcutta
Cape Town   Chennai   Dar es Salaam   Delhi   Florence   Hong Kong   Istanbul
Karachi   Kuala Lumpur   Madrid   Melbourne   Mexico City   Mumbai
Nairobi   Paris   São Paulo   Singapore   Taipei   Tokyo   Toronto   Warsaw

and associated companies in
Berlin   Ibadan

Published by Oxford University Press, Inc.
198 Madison Avenue, New York, New York 10016

Oxford is a registered trademark of Oxford University Press

Library of Congress Cataloging-in-Publication Data
Knowledge-driven work : unexpected lessons from Japanese and United
States work practices / Joel Cutcher-Gershenfeld . . . [et al.].
p.   cm. — (Japan business and economics series)
Includes bibliographical references and index.
ISBN 0-19-511454-X
1. Organizational learning—United States—Cross-cultural studies.
2. Knowledge management—United States—Cross-cultural studies.
3. Teams in the workplace—United States—Cross-cultural studies.
4. Employees—Effect of technological innovations on—United States
—Cross-cultural studies.   5. Corporations, Japanese—United States
—Management—Cross-cultural studies.   I. Cutcher-Gershenfeld, Joel.
II. Series.
HD58.82.K578   1998
658.3—dc21   98-20116

9 8 7 6 5 4 3 2 1

Printed in the United States of America
on acid-free paper

To the children of this project

The consequences of our behavior
will be returned to our children.

Foreword

· ·

Thomas A. Kochan and Haruo Shimada

Nearly thirty years ago when we, as students at the University of Wisconsin, started studying the nature of work, we did not imagine that some day we would be reconceptualizing work as "knowledge based" or that comparative analysis of employment relations would focus on cross-cultural diffusion of work systems. Nor did we expect that our students and colleagues would someday teach us about the creative potential of cross-cultural teams by studying and writing about these issues collectively.

But this is exactly what we are delighted to find in this book. It reflects the tremendous change and progress being made in the cross-cultural analysis of social and economic institutions, as well as the value to be gained from modeling this approach in thinking about the future of work, corporate organization and governance, and public policies.

We hear a great deal these days about knowledge as a source of competitive advantage. By introducing the concept of "virtual knowledge," this book appropriately focuses attention on the process by which people create knowledge—at work or elsewhere. We see the way that knowledge generation is pivotal to people's decisions about whether to change the way they do their jobs. Understanding this process opens up many new opportunities to employers and unions, including gaining insights into the cross-cultural diffusion of innovation. Leaders who do not understand or attend to these processes ignore them at their own risk.

A quick retrospective, personal journey of events that opened our eyes over the years to the importance of cross-cultural transfer of ideas and workplace practices may help put this work in perspective. In 1985, while on a sabbatical leave at MIT, Haruo Shimada teamed up with John

Paul MacDuffie, an MIT graduate student, in a series of case studies of Japanese auto plants that had recently opened in the United States. Their observations of how Japanese engineers and managers combined technology and work practices led them to coin the term "humanware." The essential insight of humanware was that the hardware dimensions of technology could not be separated from the knowledge, skills, and motivation of the workforce. Workers indeed were essential to "giving wisdom to the machines," a phrase engineers in these plants often repeated to the researchers. The insights from these cases helped launch many of the ideas that were later embedded in influential follow-on research by MacDuffie and colleagues that compared work practices in the global auto industry, which served as a precursor for what the authors describe in rich detail here as "knowledge-driven work."

Simultaneously, in the early to mid 1980s, many of us at MIT (Thomas Kochan, Harry Katz, Robert McKersie, Peter Cappelli, Michael Piore, and Charles Sabel) were busy arguing and writing about how work and industrial relations were being transformed as managers, workers, and union leaders struggled to introduce more flexible work systems and direct employee voice into their employment relationships. The challenge was originally framed as a union-nonunion comparison, but gradually variations in both union and nonunion settings dwarfed that simple distinction. This book takes us much further by demonstrating that it is not the formal work practices per se that matter most; it is the way knowledge is embedded in who does the work, and how they communicate and use that knowledge explicitly and tacitly in their everyday activities.

In the 1980s, comparisons between Japanese and U.S. work practices were the focus of attention. Today, again as this book demonstrates so clearly, we are well beyond making generalizations or simple comparisons of "national" models. Variations occur within countries, across industries and companies, and over time as succeeding generations of managers, workers, and union leaders learn from the successes and failures of their predecessors and as they innovate through adopting and adapting the ideas of others. Moreover, the path of diffusion has become more scattershot and reciprocal than a simple one-way transfer. Today, we find different features of the knowledge-based work systems in plants and offices we visit in countries as diverse as the Philippines, Australia, South Africa, Germany, France, Ireland, and Brazil. Diffusion processes, like most other economic and social ideas and institutions, respect no boundaries. They spread through the combined force of market pressures, modern communications media, and most importantly, through human interaction and learning. This makes it essential for us as scholars and teachers to do what this innovative research team did: to learn by working together and sharing the deep insights that come from mixing talented and fresh young minds representing different cultures and experience bases.

Finally, this book reflects the new model needed for discourse and analysis of public policies governing work, corporations, and labor market institutions. We come from an era in which policy was thought of as a macro-economic and political problem. Policy analysts were expected to look at macro-level interactions from above and outside the "black box" of what went on inside the firm and at the workplace. Too much policy analysis is still done this way—far removed from an understanding of the role that people and the knowledge they bring to work play in structuring organizations and employment relationships. One of the lessons of this book is that policies governing work and organizations must be shaped from the ground up—by understanding and taking into account how knowledge is mobilized, utilized, and transferred to create value, to contribute to rising standards of living, and to foster human growth and satisfaction. Over time, realization of the importance of human knowledge as an asset in corporations will reshape not only the way work is done, but also perhaps even the way corporations are governed. Efforts to remake or reform corporations, financial markets and institutions, unions, or labor market policies without taking the insights offered in this book into account are bound to fail.

For us, then, this book has provided a welcome opportunity to again work together and reflect on the changes in our field and speculate on the future. We invite you to use it for similar self-reflection. But the real value of this book will be realized if we use it as the authors used their creative research process—to learn together and use the insights derived to foster continuous innovation and improvements in how work is done, how organizations and employment relations are structured, and how public policies might be updated to allow the full potential of human knowledge to be realized in our economies and societies.

Preface

· ·

In our early visits to Japanese-affiliated factories in the United States, we saw things that were not in any of the books or articles that we had read about new work practices. We saw people making a difference in ways that challenged core assumptions about how improvement happens in an organization. We saw the early signs of what we now refer to as knowledge-driven work systems.

At first, we saw teams, technology, investment, employment security, and many other practices as distinct. In time we began to see connections. Puzzles prompted our discussion. In one setting, we would see a *kaizen* program that looked good on paper but was not matched by the same level of energy on the shop floor. We would ask ourselves why. In another setting, there might be a very simple problem-solving process but extensive problem solving taking place all the time. Again, we would ask why. Answers did not come all at once. But the series of "aha!" experiences have kept us engaged in a unique learning process.

The writing of this book reflects what we have learned from the organizations we have studied. On the Work Practices Diffusion Team, we have people from many cultures, a range of scholarly disciplines, a mix of union and management backgrounds, and a span across three generations. For example, our group has included people from Canada, Hong Kong, India, Japan, Laos, South Africa, Taiwan, Tunisia, and the United States. We span the fields of anthropology, economics, history, industrial relations, organizational behavior, psychology, religious studies, resource development, sociology, and urban studies. Included in the group are people who have been leading practitioners in organizations such as Ford and the United Auto Workers who were simultaneously pursuing graduate studies. Other group members have drawn on past work experiences in settings as diverse as the International Labor Organization, the U.S. occupation of Japan, the Indian ordnance industry, restaurant management, and the American Postal Workers Union. Writing has been as much a process of interpreting what we have seen as it has been a process of understanding the many lenses that we were using.

To build on the many perspectives and to incorporate things that many different people saw on each site visit, we found ourselves writing in a unique way. Many of us would be in a room, with one person at a keyboard and with the group heatedly discussing an issue. Bit by bit, text would be recorded on a large computer screen, edited on line, and agreed upon. Even this preface was written this way.

In this process, what we have called virtual knowledge was constantly in the air. Ideas were being proposed, challenged, adjusted, and ultimately recorded as new, explicit understandings of the group. The process has not been easy. These are issues on which we all have strong feelings. Sometimes it has taken hard confrontations to surface assumptions that some of us did not even notice we were making. Amazingly, we have kept coming back for more—we were not done learning. Of course, it helped that the group's multicultural character meant that there was always interesting food at writing sessions.

Since the project spans many years, we have struggled with the dynamics of people moving away and others joining the project. In the end, we have each had our own personal learning process, but there is also a shared foundation about a form of knowledge creation that can be quite powerful. When one of us has had to be away from the project for any period of time, that individual has had to undergo the difficult process of learning about ideas that were shared in a moment of learning. This is an issue for any knowledge-driven work system.

We hope that the ideas in this book make a difference. Along these lines, we had a conversation with a senior manager in one of our sites who had just reviewed our chapter on diffusion. He said he had taken the three diffusion strategies mentioned in the chapter and recorded them on a yellow Post-it Note, placed over his desk. The three strategies highlighted in that chapter were identified by the words "piecemeal," "imposed," and "negotiated." The manager indicated that he looks at this whenever he contemplates diffusion or any implementation of change. The three words remind him to avoid piecemeal or imposed strategies and to attend to the primary theme throughout this book, which is that people matter.

Acknowledgments

· ·

We are indebted to our families and significant others. This project has been sustained and enriched by food prepared for team meetings, birthday cakes sent in the mail, and potluck gatherings in various homes. More important, this book would not exist were it not for support during field trips in the United States and Japan, as well as an unending tolerance for countless meetings on Thursday evenings, Sunday mornings, and other times. How can we express in words our appreciation for Mary Ishino, who joined us in Japan, always had fresh baked treats for our meetings, and served as a sounding board for Dr. Ishino and many of us? How can we acknowledge the support of Hisako Inaba, who also joined us in Japan and helped us untangle the many cross-cultural puzzles that we encountered in the United States and in Japan? How can we ever know what it has taken for Anna Liza A. Armedilla, William E. Barrett, Susan Cutcher-Gershenfeld, Martha Jo Marcero, Jeannie Mothersell, Hiroko Nitta, Mary Russell, and Karen Strolle to be both sounding boards and supports over the years? Even if we can never fully answer these questions, we want at least to take this opportunity to say thank you.

This book is dedicated to the children of this project, including quite a few who were born while it was under way. In particular, we are motivated in our work by the energy and enthusiasm of Amanda, Jonathan, and Alexandria, Christina and Jenna, Daniel and Justin, Eric and Lee, Fred, Gabriel and Aaron, Jessica and Kirsten, Lin Yen-Ju and Lee Yi-Jeng, Lyssa, Natalie and Robert, Ryo and Yumi, and Aditya, Sahana, Viditya, and Anant.

Though some of the original members of the project have moved on, we are deeply appreciative of their many contributions. These include Kevin Small, Cheryl Coutchie, Stacia Rabine, and Seepa Lee.

Throughout this journey we have had the privilege of sharing our ideas with numerous colleagues around the world, from whom we have received invaluable encouragement and feedback. Some have joined us for team meetings or writing sessions, others have hosted us at seminars, and still others have commented on draft portions of the manuscript. These include Paul Adler, Toshikata Amino, Mark Anstey, Greg Bamber, Alan Gruner, Mitsuo Ishida, Toru Kiyomiya, Thomas Kochan, Keisuke Nakamura, Yoshifumi Nakata, Mitsumasa Onitsuka and Masako Onitsuka, Dong Ok Lee, Raj Ramanand, Sam Seites, Haruo Shimada, Kenichi Shinohara, John Van Maanen, Eleanor Westney, and Elaine Yakura.

We have presented our findings in over a dozen seminars and conferences. The discussions and comments at these sessions have been invaluable. In particular we want to express our appreciation to participants in sessions held at the Association of Japanese Business Studies in New York (1993), Michigan State University (1994, 1995, and 1996), the Institute for Social Science in the University of Tokyo (1994), the International Industrial Relations Association in Washington (1995) and Taipei (1996), the Work in America Institute seminars in New York (1995) and Tokyo (1996), St. Andrews University in Osaka (1996), Doshisha University in Kyoto (1996), the Industrial Relations Seminar at MIT (1996), the University of Illinois Conference in Chicago (1996), and MIT's Lean Aerospace Initiative Research Seminar (1998).

Funds supporting this project have been made possible by many people in organizations in the United States and in Japan. We are grateful for the hospitality of the staff and leadership at the Japan Center for Michigan Universities, located in Shiga, Japan. Funds from the Matsushita Foundation supported our travel in Japan and are deeply appreciated. Members of our team received individual support in their travels from UAW Local 602 and the Ford Motor Company. The support from many parts of Michigan State University has been both essential and motivating, including funding through the School of Labor and Industrial Relations (SLIR), the College of Social Science, the Graduate School, the International Studies Program, and the Center for International Business Education and Research. Among the leaders and key individuals facilitating this support from across MSU are Tamer Cavusgill, Dean Kenneth Corey, Dean Gil Chin Lim, Sandra Gleason, Ed Graham, Karen Klomparens, Myron Miller, and Michael Moore.

How can we express our appreciation to the many people we have met in the organizations we visited? We have listed here the names of those who have spent special time with us on our visits, many of whom have continued to correspond about chapter drafts and other matters. These include Bill Childs, Charlie Curry, Michael Damer, Jerry Dunn, Jim Edgar,

Mike Gagnon, Steve Hara, Norimitsu Hayakawa, Mike Hoffman, Bill Hollister, Phil Keeling, Jay Kyogoku, Dave Leisman, Mitsuko Marx, Michiro Morita, Haruya Murakoshi, Clyde Nash, George Nano, John Nielsen, Tokio Ogihara, Ken Ohashi, Dr. Nancy Henninger Reisig, Hideo Soneoka, Stan Tooley, and Jesse Wyngard. Our thanks also go to Annette Bacon and Janice Trudgeon, SLIR staff, for assisting us in many ways. Last but not least, our appreciation and thanks go to the Oxford University Press staff who helped us bring this book to fruition: Herbert Addison, MaryBeth Branigan, and copyeditor David Severtson. Finally, we are appreciative of the many others whose knowledge is driving these various workplaces, who were kind enough to share some of their wisdom with us, and who demonstrated great hospitality that we only hope to be able to return in the years to come.

Contents

· ·

KNOWLEDGE-DRIVEN WORK

1

Details Matter

· ·

This book began as a study of shop-floor work practices in Japanese-affiliated plants in North America. We were initially drawn to the study of these work practices for all the usual reasons,[1] including the importance of the global economy and the Japanese reputation for quality and productivity. Reports in the literature suggested that work practices in Japanese-affiliated factories would be very different and highly productive. These expectations began to shift even before our initial plant visits. Some managers said that we would be welcome to come study their factories but that we should know in advance that we wouldn't find a stereotypical Japanese workplace. As we visited the companies we saw that they indeed did not fit stereotypes. Instead, there was a much more complex and puzzling story that was unfolding.

It soon became evident that we would be writing an unconventional book on Japanese work practices. We found ourselves talking to North American workers and managers who were learning new practices and did so with a combination of pride and frustration as they integrated them into their own way of working. These practices could be found in parent facilities in Japan, but unique variations were occurring as they were adopted in the United States. We were fortunate in being able to talk with Japanese managers and engineers who had returned to Japan after assignments in the United States. These returnees went back to Japan full of new ideas and experiences. We now see that the flow of work practices from Japan to North America and from North America back to Japan is a single case of a much larger global process of work practice diffusion.[2]

It is important to examine the diffusion of work practices for reasons that reach far beyond debates over the merits or limitations of Japa-

3

nese manufacturing systems. These debates have typically centered on technical issues such as the value of just-in-time (JIT) delivery or the cost and quality advantages of reduced in-process inventory or the efficiency of simultaneous engineering. Our analysis urges that the resolution of these debates requires a focus on people as well as technical considerations. For example, reduced in-process inventory depends on continuous improvement in operations, which is driven, in turn, by people's knowledge, ideas, and suggestions. Similarly, simultaneous engineering succeeds in producing better designs on a speedier basis only where dozens of interdependent design teams are able to work cooperatively, independently, and even competitively. We recognized early on that human interactions at all levels of the firm were as vital as technology.

A key finding in this book is that the massive global diffusion of work practices rests on a fragile foundation.[3] This is the process by which individuals and groups of people come to new understandings concerning the adoption of new work practices. This diffusion process centers on the generation and sharing of knowledge.

"Knowledge" and "learning" are two of the most frequently used words in modern organizational literature.[4] They are typically discussed in highly theoretical pieces or in work focused at executive or managerial "leadership" levels. However, we found that knowledge and learning occur with equal importance at the shop-floor level. In particular, we emphasize one form of knowledge, which we have termed virtual knowledge. Specifically, we define virtual knowledge as a moment of shared understanding—an "aha!"—that is sparked by purposeful, individual, and collective interactions. It is a moment of standardization in a dynamic group process, where tacit knowledge becomes explicit in ways that can be applied.

Explicit knowledge is often tangible. It is found in manuals, books, policies, procedures, work rules, engineering drawings, and collective bargaining agreements. Tacit knowledge is harder to see or touch. It is found in the shared problem-solving techniques, symbols, metaphors, and unique meanings enacted by members of a specific organization. It can only be shared on a person-to-person basis. Virtual knowledge is created as individually held tacit knowledge is shared among a group of people who will develop it into explicit knowledge as they work toward solving a problem.

Consider the case of a group of people who are beginning to understand how to apply statistical process control (SPC) principles in their work area. The adoption of the technical practice of SPC depends on the success of their initial conversations and the group's interpretation of some preliminary experiments with the process. This movement from tacit to explicit knowledge helps individuals share sensemaking and problem solving as they face ambiguous situations.[5] While explicit knowledge is easier to observe, it is the virtual knowledge that we believe activates the innovation processes that help align organizations and unleash competitive advantage.

The decision to introduce new work practices across cultures is a strategic one. For many years, it was typical for firms to adopt local practices for selection, training, compensation, supervision, maintenance, work organization, and collective bargaining. Even today, a great deal of investment occurs in this way. However, something more is required for organizations that attempt to transfer entire production systems that they see as the key to their global business strategy. These organizations are faced with a difficult array of questions. Cultural difference heightens the difficulties of setting up a knowledge-driven work system.

There are many types of knowledge-driven work systems. In production operations, for example, we explore both lean production and the sociotechnical systems (STS) forms of knowledge-driven work systems. These work systems contrast directly with a mass production and bureaucratic model, in which expertise is assumed to be at progressively higher levels of organizations. By contrast, a knowledge-driven work system is rooted in the assumption that key expertise lies at all levels of the organization and its corollary, that continuous improvement at any level can be driven only by the people with the relevant knowledge.

Thus, the knowledge-creation process—building on virtual knowledge—is essential in global diffusion. Furthermore, it is a particular type of work system—one that is knowledge driven—that is most important in the present era.

In the process of global diffusion, we have come to see just how much people and details matter. This view directly challenges a form of technical benchmarking that is all too common. A leading manufacturer is identified and the technical features of its work systems are held up as best practice to be duplicated. Despite the many technical accomplishments to be found in Japanese manufacturing operations in North America, we believe that the deeper lessons concern the channeling of the knowledge of thousands of individuals around tens of thousands of detailed work practices. These people, their work practices, and the shared knowledge they construct are the leading edge of a global transformation.

Lean Production and the Machine That Changed the World

This project began in direct response to the widely read MIT study *The Machine That Changed the World*, which focused on what the authors termed lean production as an emerging alternative to mass production.[6] The book offered a compelling story about new manufacturing methods but did not tell us enough about the impact of these new methods on the people, employment relations policies, and broader patterns of human interaction in these settings.[7]

At the outset, we knew that the lean production concept was controversial. Some have termed it "management by stress."[8] Under lean production principles, the focus is on removing buffers in an organization (such as in-process inventories) and eliminating waste (including material scrap, excess energy utilization, and extra motions by operators).[9] Critics of lean production point to the human costs of work intensification: lost recovery time for specific operations, lost autonomy from having movements standardized and charted in increments of a few seconds, and lost co-workers as a result of process improvements are some of these costs.

We knew that "people issues" were a key point of controversy in debates over lean production. We suspected that people were also the key to success in lean production. Though the point is not discussed in great detail in the literature, we were quite certain that people (not just technology) were driving the process of continuous improvement. We were also increasingly persuaded that the concept of lean production was interwoven with the idea of continuous improvement in operations. We didn't think that people would sustain continuous improvement solely out of fear in a high-stress context, but there was little discussion about what features of the new manufacturing methods might be motivating or engaging.

Too many North American managers have been drawn to the concept of lean production as a vehicle for cutting costs and reducing staff—confirming the suspicions of critics of lean production. In our observations and research, we have found these concepts to be much more complex. In fact, where lean production is utilized with the aim of cutting cost through cutting staff, it will undercut people's motivation to contribute their ideas and energies. Reducing the number of people associated with a particular task may be a by-product, but without full attention to all the elements of continuous improvement, knowledge just ends up walking out of the firm.

This is part of a longer history in the United States of focusing only on the superficial or tangible features of new work practices. The first reaction to Japanese quality systems, for example, was to import one tangible feature—the quality circle—and a few tools, such as SPC and supplier audits, rather than the underlying principles. In the subsequent focus on entire work systems we again see a tendency to import only the tangible features such as teams, JIT delivery, and suggestion systems.

To understand the limited impact of quality circles, consider the context in which they operated in Japan. One piece of this context is captured by the Japanese concept called *Hoshin Kanri*. The phrase roughly translates as "policy deployment" and refers to the systematic way that broad company visions and goals are implemented with increasing specificity at each lower level of the organization. Embedded in this concept is the notion that people at all levels need to have specific competencies and capabilities to translate the broad goals and visions into the work they do. Furthermore, this is not just a top-down control mechanism, but rather a framework within which ideas and knowledge can be used most effectively. It has the effect of fostering increased competency at all levels of a workplace. In this regard, a quality circle is not an isolated innovation, but an integral component in a management system.

In our examination of the beneficial and the negative implications of lean production and other types of knowledge-driven work systems, the focus will be on the people in these systems. We will be exploring how people are integral to continuous improvement and how they are also at risk in increasingly lean operations.

The Transformation of American Industrial Relations

In the field of industrial relations, a lively debate is under way regarding the degree to which a transformation is occurring in union–management relations. In their book *The Transformation of American Industrial Relations*, Kochan, Katz, and McKersie point out that since the 1980s the nonunion sector has played a major role in setting the agenda for the unionized sector—a reversal of historical U.S. patterns for the prior 30 years.[10]

Specifically, the nonunion sector has framed the agenda for the unionized sector in its focus on reducing the costs of benefits, alternative forms of compensation, increased flexibility in work practices, and new vehicles for employee voice. Consequently, fundamental challenges are posed for unions, their members, and even management counterparts in unionized locations. We suspect that the Japanese operations—whether unionized or not—are somehow also part of the landscape of transformation in industrial relations.

It was with these ideas in mind that we initially selected a mix of unionized and nonunion settings and even oversampled the unionized sector. We were mindful that some Japanese firms have entered into joint ventures where unionized workforces were maintained while others have aggressively sought to retain nonunion status. We were also aware that there is a different model of unionization in large manufacturing operations in Japan.[11]

As with many other aspects of this project, the issue of union status in the Japanese-affiliated locations proved far more complex and nuanced than we anticipated. For example, we initially assumed that some North American–Japanese factories were located in rural settings as part of a union avoidance strategy. We did find that many Japanese firms were concerned over how to work with North American unions. Yet their motivations in choosing rural locations also reflected a view common in the U.S. nonunion sector. A rural workforce is seen as more highly motivated, more adaptable to new work practices, and more homogenous. Moreover, labor costs are often lower in more rural locations, and these communities are bidding aggressively (with tax and training incentives) to attract plants.[12] Additionally, the distinction between union and nonunion facilities proved less salient than a distinction we found between North American investments made prior to 1980 and in the years since—a finding discussed in more detail in chapter 4. Thus, the comparison between union and nonunion Japanese facilities in North America raises issues that reach far beyond questions of union avoidance.

In this sense, the experience in these Japanese-affiliated manufacturing firms is not just an extension of the union and nonunion domestic transformation debate. Our experience points to a reinterpretation and broadening of research on the transformation of U.S. industrial relations. Flexibility, communication, and coordination in these locations, union and nonunion, are parts of a larger transformation story. Competitors of these firms are adjusting work practices in response to the perceived advantages of the Japanese-affiliated facilities as they are forced to compete with these firms.

Employees—workers and managers—are moving from these firms to other domestic locations and bringing ideas and practices with them. Neighboring facilities are learning about new practices through informal community networks and direct ties through community colleges and other mechanisms. Ideas are moving upstream and downstream through supplier and customer links. Finally, the overall climate that emphasizes benchmarking and competitive response drives an emphasis on learning from the experiences in these Japanese-affiliated locations.

All told, the resulting transformation in work practices and industrial relations far exceeds the story that Kochan, Katz, and McKersie told about union and nonunion sectors. Indeed, we are left with an overwhelming sense of the scale and scope of change associated with the global diffusion of work practices.

Technology and Capital Investment

Communities across the world are seeking capital investment and new technology as vehicles for job creation and growth. This is a key driving force in the global diffusion of work practices. For example, at least 39 U.S. states and countless other nations have established offices in Tokyo to solicit capital investment.[13]

Our group's initial field research focused on issues of technology and capital investment, along with a lengthy list of work-practice topics such as worker participation, training, recruitment, selection, compensation, employment security, communication, dispute resolution, and union–management relations. Our interest in technology and capital investment reflected a traditional view in which these factors are seen as primary sources of competitive advantage.

Early on in the project, however, we found that the answers to questions about technology and capital investment pointed to a complex mix of meanings that were attached to equipment and facilities. For example, the new metal stamping facility that Ogihara built in Howell, Michigan, takes on particular meaning given that Ogihara in Japan is not in the metal stamping business. This plant represented an experimental entry in a new line of business. Similarly, the new continuous steel processing technology at I/NTek near South Bend, Indiana, had direct implications for work-group structure and operations. Thus, we stopped asking separate questions about technology and capital investment. Instead, we began to see the ways in which capital investment and technology were interwoven into our questions on all the other work practices.

There is a long-standing debate in the literature over the degree to which technology is deterministic. At one extreme, some scholars have argued that certain kinds of technology point to certain predictable outcomes. For example, it has been argued that mass production technologies are essentially dehumanizing while new information technologies inevitably facilitate the flow of information. Some scholars have challenged these views, seeing technology as more contextual in its meaning.[14] Our research builds on this alternative perspective.

The increasingly integrated view of technology and capital investment reflects a broader lesson from the research, which involves the degree to which all aspects of a production system are interrelated. The work system and the technology cannot be fully understood without attention to people, training, union–management relations, and interaction processes. In fact, the whole concept of capital investment takes on a meaning much broader than money spent on equipment and facilities—expanding to include investment in the selection, training, and development of the workforce.

Our findings go beyond the notion of a balance between the technical and social dimensions, however. It is perhaps no surprise that we come down solidly on the side of people—emphasizing the overarching importance of people having the capability to ensure that the technological potential is realized. It is the diffusion of these intangible capabilities, much more than the tangible work practices or technical systems, that represents the key source of competitive advantage.

Cross-Cultural Diffusion

At the outset of this project, we had what we now understand to be a simplistic and overly mechanistic view of diffusion. It is only a slight overstatement to say that we imagined specific practices such as employment security policies, team work structures, and compensation systems that would have been either imported from Japan or adopted out of the U.S. context. Certainly, much of the literature treats work practices in this way.

Early in the project, however, we were joined by a cultural anthropologist who led a special group session on the concepts of cross-cultural diffusion.[15] The session highlighted two key insights.[16] First, we saw that cross-cultural diffusion inevitably involves intended and unintended consequences.[17] For example, when Columbus came to North America there were a number of unintended consequences such as the diffusion of diseases from Europe to North America and then back to Europe.[18] This concept immediately resonated with our initial field findings, since we heard so many stories about unexpected lessons. There were technical lessons such as new discoveries about metal stamping going back to Japan. There were also administrative lessons such as the application of Japanese open office arrangements. For example, at one firm we observed management labor relations representatives and elected union committeepersons sharing desks, phones, and office space. Social lessons also emerged, such as two-way culinary learning in plant cafeterias.[19]

The second insight from the literature concerns the way in which work practices are embedded in larger cultural contexts. As a result, any practice that is transferred can change in at least three ways. It can change due to being extracted from a given culture. It can change by virtue of who is transferring the practice and how they do so. And it can change as a result of the new host setting. For example, the concept of employment security in Japan is embedded in a set of cultural assumptions about continuity of employment as well as an economic context involving a labor market structure featuring a core and a periphery. When the concept was introduced in some of the firms we visited, the use of temporary workers (as a buffer for good and bad economic times) was also introduced. An attempt was also made to accommodate the cultural traditions regarding continuity of employment by selecting employees who were expected to be highly attached to the firm. In fact, the resulting mix of practices varies from site to site—reflecting a different set of larger common cultural drivers—and none of the practices functions exactly as they do in Japan. This, in turn, surfaces new learning about what we now see as emerging social contracts between employers and employees in these settings.

These two insights about cross-cultural diffusion directly contrast with traditional notions of planned change. While many of our sites do reflect the intentional transfer of Japanese practices or local adoption of North American work practices, they also feature countless instances of unexpected learning and the impact of multiple cultural contexts. The resulting picture is not one of a discrete set of "Japanese" practices lifted out of one culture and dropped on another. Instead, it is of a highly complex, negotiated process put into operation in a diverse range of communities and workforces. Many different bundles of practices are transferred, and whether they are transferred is based on the interactions of multiple different stakeholders with diverse intentions. The initial reaction of many North American manufacturers is to treat lean production as a unitary phenomenon, despite the diversity of practices in Japan and the range of ways in which they can be brought to this country.

Rather than seeing cross-cultural diffusion as a linear, mechanistic process in which one or a few practices are moved from one culture to another, we now see it as a complex dynamic.[20] We see work practices that are utilized in integrated, parallel, and independent ways, and these variations have consequences for all parties involved. We also see this as a dynamic, negotiated process among the various stakeholders—where the negotiations concern the interpretation and use of new ideas or work practices.[21] Thus, we are confident in predicting that the ultimate impact of these work practices will be felt in ways that are as yet unknown and unpredictable.

Emerging Social Contracts

Traditionally, a dominant social norm in the United States is that people do eight hours' work for eight hours' pay—a quid pro quo that focuses on a substantive contract between the individual and his or her employer. During our visits to some Japanese-affiliated facilities, we encountered a farther-reaching and more complex set of mutual understandings, which we are referring to as social contracts.[22]

Emerging social contracts seem to involve a set of reciprocal obligations and commitments that employers and employees each take on. Employees in some of the firms we visited expressed a willingness to work hard and contribute ideas toward continuous improvement. Equally, these same employees expressed a high level of confidence in their employer's concern for their needs. We asked employees at Denso Manufacturing–Michigan, Inc., and Ogihara, "What will happen when you get older and can't work in the same way?" One response at Denso Manufacturing–Michigan, Inc., was that "the company will take care of that." We heard a similar response at Ogihara. In fact, some company executives indicated that they are exploring long-term job redesign to attend to the shifting physical capabilities of an aging workforce. The employees' confidence in their employers seemed almost naive, except that these individuals reported a concrete foundation for their views—this was a work system, they pointed out, in which people were instrumental to success. These people were not blindly accepting the "official" lines. Rather, they believed in what they were experiencing and creating on a daily basis.

Interestingly, the strength of these emerging social contracts was comparable in unionized and nonunion companies. In both cases, there was a level of commonality in views across individual employees. People would point to instances that would have led to layoffs with past employers where their present Japanese employer assigned "excess" workers to training and development activities. The commonality of views represented a collective force very different from what we associate with collective bargaining. In this context, unions found themselves less able to derive power by withholding work. Instead, they were beginning to fashion ways to exercise power by enabling work.

The emerging social contracts seemed a powerful force but also a complicated one in the U.S. context. The use of temporary workers is a major factor enabling the social contracts featuring high levels of employment security in many of the firms we visited. These temporary workers often work with the hope of entering the core workforce. We found that the full-time workers had difficulty reconciling the two contrasting levels of status—especially when the temporary workers had fewer options, despite working side by side.[23]

It is difficult to predict the long-term implications of these emerging social contracts. We are confident, however, that they will take on meanings that differ from the reciprocal understanding either in Japan or the United States. It will be most interesting to see the impact of this another set of social contracts on employment relationships in both nations. In this sense, we are bearing witness to a process in which social contracts are being constructed and renegotiated—with both intended and unintended outcomes—all fitting together as part of a complex, global adaptive system.[24]

Virtual Knowledge and Organizational Learning

We did not begin the project looking at issues of organizational learning or knowledge creation. However, the concepts of knowledge creation and learning emerged as central to the phenomena we are studying. At its root, learning involves interactions—where there is a sender, a receiver, and a process through which information is assimilated. The term "virtual knowledge" was coined during the course of writing this book as we tried to explain what we were observing.[25] Certainly, we found ourselves documenting countless instances of such exchanges, each of which generated various forms of knowledge.

Many of the exchanges were planned—what might be called intentional learning. For example, the New United Motor Manufacturing Inc. (NUMMI) plant in Fremont, California, is a product of a planned two-way learning exchange. Toyota hoped to learn about the degree to which its production system would (or would not) flourish with a North American workforce and supplier network. It sought a joint venture arrangement with General Motors in order to minimize the financial risk associated with learning this lesson. General Motors hoped to learn more about the Toyota production system (and its viability in a North American setting), which drove its interest in a joint venture with Toyota.

Similarly, the Ogihara facility in Howell, Michigan, represented an intentional learning experiment in that Ogihara was entering a new line of business (it is a leading die maker in Japan, but not in the metal stamping business). The Coil Center Corporation is an experiment in that the Japanese partner, Tomen, is a large trading company and its movement into metal stamping of auto components is also a movement into a new line of business.

Beyond the strategic learning in these cases, there were also many instances of intentional learning woven into day-to-day operations. Many of our sites emphasized worker training and education. In one organization, for example, staffing plans were based on the assumption that about 5% of the workforce would always be off the job and attending training of one kind or another. Another form of intentional learning can be found in the extensive benchmarking activities across these sites. When these organizations implement a new process or technology, it is now routine for them to identify and study "best-in-class" organizations regarding this particular process or technology.[26]

A third form of intentional learning lies in the detailed supplier certification processes that most of our sites are subject to and that nearly all impose on their suppliers. These certification procedures establish clear criteria for quality, cost, schedule, and a host of operating practices (such as the use of SPC), and they provide learning mechanisms to enable suppliers to meet the criteria.

Finally, the continuous improvement processes in many of our sites are organized around formal employee involvement and suggestion programs—termed *kaizen-teian* systems in some cases.[27] These kaizen initiatives are an intentional form of learning in that new ideas are sought through the collection and interpretation of data—a planned learning and training process. In fact, people in kaizen-oriented systems have been termed "knowledge workers."[28] We have highlighted the process for creating this knowledge in our use of the term "virtual knowledge."

Just on the basis of all these instances of intentional learning, it is clear that organizational learning frameworks have potential utility for the study of Japanese-affiliated facilities in North America. However, the importance of the concept is further heightened if we recall one of the two major lessons about cross-cultural diffusion—the inevitability of unintended consequences. Our field notes are full of instances of unintentional learning examples. Learning occurred, for instance, when a female team leader from one of our sites was sent for advanced training to Japan at a location where the team leader role is held only by male workers. Confusion resulted on details concerning status (such as whether she should be served sake, an honor usually reserved for men), lodging in company dormitories, and other aspects of her visit. It is likely that neither the parent organization in Japan nor the initial U.S. workforce ever anticipated this sort of learning opportunity.

A far-reaching example of unintended learning lies in the redrafting of Toyota's corporate guiding principles based on experiences at NUMMI and in other settings around the globe. The new draft, which reflects a more globally decentralized and culturally sensitive corporate stance, reads as follows:

Guiding Principles at Toyota

1. Be a company of the world.
2. Serve the greater good of people everywhere by devoting careful attention to safety and to the environment.
3. Assert leadership in technology and in customer satisfaction.
4. Become a contributing member of the community in every nation.

5. Foster a corporate culture that honors individuality while promoting teamwork.
6. Pursue continuing growth through efficient, global management.
7. Build a lasting relationship with business partners around the world.[29]

We were told this was rewritten by senior executives after some had completed assignments at NUMMI and other locations outside of Japan.

Finally, as Japanese executives and engineers have returned to Japan they and their families have brought back a host of lessons around issues of schooling, gender roles, community, individuality, and other matters. While many of these individuals may downplay these new thoughts upon their return to Japan (so as not to appear too different), there are likely to be many long-term implications of these new lessons.

The concept of unintended learning underlies the title of this chapter—details matter. It is in countless details that we find evidence for the many forms of unintended learning. Further, the mechanism for this learning is this ephemeral phenomenon of virtual knowledge. As we noted at the beginning of the chapter, we use the term "virtual knowledge" to refer to the sets of understandings that emerge in the course of interactions within groups of people. It is knowledge that is not yet codified in the form of tacit or explicit understandings. If the group energy or membership shifts or is disrupted, the ideas and understandings inevitably change. It is in this sense that we have called the knowledge "virtual"—it exists only in the moment among the group of people engaged in dialogue.

This knowledge does not reside in any one individual, and it is not fully captured in manuals, policy documents, contracts, or other records. Though the knowledge itself is hard to identify, its impact can be seen in the way in which groups and even organizations anticipate and respond to events. This has parallels to what physicists term "virtual particles," which cannot be observed but which have observable effects.[30] Similarly, the growing popularity of "virtual reality" refers to situations in which simulations produce effects that are experienced as real.

There is also a growing literature on "virtual organizations," which refers to organizations that exist through a network of interactions rather than a specific organizational form. Pulling on these diverse images, we are coming to refer to the shared knowledge as virtual knowledge since it is hard to observe in itself but its effects can be powerful. The knowledge is considered virtual since it is not any one individual's knowledge but rather a set of understandings that exists only to the extent that the group or organization continues to maintain and attend to the knowledge base. Furthermore, where there are changes in the composition of the group or organization, the virtual knowledge changes—since it now rests on a different mix of interactions and memories. Virtual knowledge can expand, shrink, or otherwise shift with changes in the mix of people involved.

For example, the workers at Denso Manufacturing–Michigan, Inc., maintain written logs in which they record their machines' maintenance, performance, and other particular events (such as anomalous noises) during a given shift. To reinforce the recording in the logs, there are posted signs with pictures of eyes, ears, and noses, emphasizing the use of all senses. While many organizations have policies of maintaining written logs, this practice at Denso Manufacturing–Michigan, Inc., triggers the creation of virtual knowledge when people actually use the logs and talk about what is in them. As conversations lead to formal problem solving, the virtual knowledge becomes explicit knowledge in the form of implemented suggestions for improvement.

Changes in virtual knowledge can occur as a result of planned interventions (such as hiring new workers or planned job rotation) or as a result of unplanned events (such as an unexpected machine failure). Either way, the virtual knowledge that emerges cannot be fully anticipated. Thus, an unexpected consequence of employment security assurances is the emergence of a body of virtual knowledge, which itself is constantly evolving.

It is important to note that virtual knowledge is constructed in a variety of ways. It can include formal group meetings, but it can also include a group of employees talking heatedly in a break room or in a union grievance committee meeting or managers planning the launch of a new initiative. The knowledge emerges in reaction to a commonly perceived situation but can take many different paths.

We are coming to the conclusion that attention to details and appreciation for the knowledge-generation process best accounts for variation across Japanese-affiliated facilities. We observed some organizations that are elevating these principles to be core elements of their business strategy—resulting in an exceptional level of appreciation for the power and importance of knowledge-driven work.

Conclusion

This book reports on a unique journey by a multidisciplinary, cross-cultural group of scholars. We began with a simple idea, which was tracing work practices from Japan and the United States in a mix of Japanese-affiliated factories in North America. Early on, we recognized that it was going to be a long journey—and we are still not done.

Along the way, we encountered countless individuals who reported that their personal lives have changed as a result of working in these workplaces. They were rethinking assumptions on everything from the way they chopped vegetables to the way they raised their children. We too have been changed as a result of our travels. In sharing the lessons of our research, we are inviting our readers to join us in the journey.

In extending this invitation, we are mindful of the complex nature of the journey. To use colloquial language, most North American managers who visit Japanese-affiliated factories or that hear about Japanese methods just don't get it. They look for the pieces of the work system that they might benchmark and adopt—without examining their fundamental assumptions about organizations and the role of people at work.

Yet in our study of the establishment of Japanese work systems in North America the clearest lesson is that specific work practices are less important than an overall approach to work. A particular way of assuring preventive maintenance is less important than a capacity to foster continuous improvement in maintenance practices. In our research, we met countless individuals who are working in these factories and who are at various stages of making sense of their new work systems. To learn about these systems, one should recognize just how long the learning takes for people who work in these settings every day.

What we today see as the "Japanese" system is the product of over three decades of continuous improvement in Japan. Now there has been nearly another decade of parallel co-evolution unfolding in the Japanese-affiliated locations in North America.

By tracing the cross-cultural exchange of work practices between Japan and North America, we are afforded a window into the way these complex organizations adapt and evolve in a volatile global marketplace.[31] What we see in that window is at once powerful and fragile. The work systems are powerful in their capability to achieve quality, schedule, cost, and safety objectives, but they are fragile in their dependence on virtual knowledge as the vehicle for channeling the wisdom and motivation of workers.[32]

Most important, the experience with Japanese work practices emerges as a special case of a global process. The particular features of the Japanese system—with its focus on the frontline employee as the primary source of added value—has helped to illuminate the concept of virtual knowledge. The individual thoughts and decisions of frontline employees in countries around the world may seem like small details in something so vast as the global economy. However, to realize the full advantages of new work systems, these are details that matter.

2

Initial Visits to Japanese Factories

· ·

The production floor layout and the quality of environment in which people work is often taken for granted. Many Americans work in factories that are dirty, dangerous, noisy, cluttered, and oppressive. While people may not like these conditions, they do not usually see themselves as having the opportunity or the need to change their circumstances. Many people just focus on the small area of floor space in which they work and see the other physical aspects of their workplace as the responsibility of maintenance, engineering, custodians, or others. Most important of all, they often do not have a clear conception of what alternatives might look like or how these physical circumstances relate to matters of safety, quality, efficiency, or even psychological well-being.

Many Japanese factories based in the United States present a very different picture. The shop floor is often clean, relatively quiet, orderly, open, safe, and well lit. Relevant information is immediately visible (including performance data, locations for tools, and training accomplishments). Landscaped gardens, recreational areas, and even a fishing pond may be visible from parts of the factory. There are still hard, repetitive jobs to be done. But the physical setting sends a number of key messages to the people who work in the factory—that the people and what they produce are important and valued. Indeed, over time a message is sent to others in the community that a factory need not be a dirty, oppressive, or unsafe place to work. What would account for this contrast? In part, the cleanliness and orderliness of the Japanese factories are functions of the fact that many are new facilities. New U.S. facilities are also clean and orderly. But there is more to the story.

Careful attention to physical layout can be found in a number of older plants that are now being run under Japanese management. Managers in these plants point to very functional business reasons for the clean and orderly layout. For example, reduced in-process inventory and JIT delivery practices result in less inventory cluttering floor space. Similarly, in-station process quality control and preventive maintenance practices result in jobs in which routine cleaning is a part of a worker's duties. In fact, cleanliness and orderliness are fundamental elements of the larger production process. But even these practices do not tell the entire story.

Throughout this project, we began to see an idea that was new to us. When we visited workplaces in Japan we learned that the factory is considered almost a community to which workers belong. As such, it is deserving of the same care and pride that people might give to their homes and neighborhoods. These concepts are deeply rooted in the way people live, so some work practices associated with cleanliness and orderliness are, in effect, overdetermined—they are supported by the demands of the technical work system, but they are also consistent with social norms that people bring into the workplace.

Thus, seeing a cleaner, safer, and more attractive workplace raises a deceptively simple question—why is it different? We see that there are many layers of practices and ideas, ranging from bottom-line business practices to deep cultural traditions, that help to explain why these factories are physically attractive places to work.

In this book, we often attempt to answer deceptively simple questions about why things are as they are. Indeed, consistent with Taiichi Ohno's methods, we asked "why" multiple times (he recommends the five whys—with the fifth why getting to root causes, not symptoms or surface features).[1] To provide a context for these discussions, we will move beyond the general discussion of the physical qualities of Japanese-affiliated factories in North America and provide specific details on the layout and feel of the eight factories that we studied.

These descriptions seek to provide more than a context for thinking about the sites. The picture obtained in the course of a plant visit is part of a larger whole. Describing these visible features will help to explain other, less visible, but related features of the organizations. For example, we pay close attention to the way plant cafeterias look and even to the food provided. This does not just reflect our team's bias for interesting food. It also reflects serious research interest in cafeterias as a common meeting ground that spans organizational levels and cultural traditions. Indeed, common cafeterias are often held up by these organizations as tangible symbols of egalitarian values since many traditional factories feature separate executive cafeterias.

Conceptual Distinctions among Research Sites

From a distance, many things often appear simple. Our first ideas about what we would find at the sites we visited were relatively uncomplicated. For example, we wondered whether the sites would be different if they were unionized or not. There were questions about how a brownfield, or established, facility might look in comparison to a newer greenfield site. After our first visit, we knew that the descriptions we were constructing had to provide more than a context for thinking about the sites. We needed to develop a picture that made the details observed in a plant visit part of a larger whole.

As table 2.1 indicates, there is a great deal of diversity among our sites. They range in size from a small metal stamping plant with under 100 employees to a large auto assembly operation with over 4,500 employees. Additionally, they vary in age from over 20 years to less than five years. The sites also represent different forms of manufacturing, ranging from a cold-roll steel mill to auto assembly plants to a musical instruments factory. Still, there are important similarities among the sites. For example, two are auto assembly plants and four are auto parts supply plants. Also, all but one are located in the Midwest. Finally, though perhaps obvious, it should be noted that they are all either wholly owned subsidiaries of Japanese corporations or U.S.–Japanese joint ventures.

The sites were initially selected to achieve variety across the dimensions of size and union status. While we did not select the sites on the basis of age or work system, these factors surfaced as key distinctions in our analysis. The mix of cases includes a larger proportion of unionized sites and auto-related locations than exist in the full population of Japanese-affiliated facilities in North America. We utilize the cases for what can be thought of as hypothesis generation—surfacing important patterns and new insights. From our own experience in many other locations, we are confident that the propositions and understandings presented in this book are generalizable. Still, the reader is urged to treat these cases as instructive, not definitive.

While demographic information on the cases is important for understanding the sorts of facilities from which we are drawing our conclusions, these data do not in themselves convey all that should be said about the research sites. Beyond the numbers and classifications, each plant represents a unique community of people who go about their business in a distinctive setting.

In each of the following descriptions, we will reach beyond the descriptive numbers to give a sense of the physical site. We will do this by reviewing some of the details from our initial visits to each plant. We

Table 2.1 Descriptive Characteristics of Research Sites

Research sites	Location	Union status	Ownership and year production began	Number of employees	Primary products
AAI	Flat Rock, Mich.	UAW	Ford/Mazda* joint venture (1983 as Mazda; 1992 as AAI)	3,500	Auto assembly
Coil Center Corporation	Howell, Mich.	Nonunion	Tomen/Kasle joint venture (1991)	50	Metal blanking
Hitachi Magnetics Corporation	Edmore, Mich.	UAW	Hitachi Metals, Ltd. subsidiary (1973)	523	Permanent magnets
I/NTek	South Bend, Ind.	USWA	Inland/Nippon Steel joint venture (1990)	290	Cold-rolled steel
NUMMI	Fremont, Calif.	UAW	Toyota/GM joint venture (1984)	4,500	Auto assembly and stamping
Denso Manufacturing–Michigan, Inc.	Battle Creek, Mich.	Nonunion	Nippondenso,** Ltd. subsidiary (1986)	1,204	Auto parts
Ogihara	Howell, Mich.	Nonunion	Ogihara*** subsidiary (1986)	370	Metal stamping
Yamaha Musical Products	Grand Rapids, Mich.	UAW	Yamaha subsidiary (1973)	250	Musical instruments

*The Auto Alliance International plant at Flat Rock, Michigan, was originally wholly owned by Mazda Japan, and production began in 1983 at the Mazda Flat Rock plant. It became a joint venture with Ford in 1992.

**Nippondenso Manufacturing U.S.A. has changed its name to Denso Manufacturing–Michigan, Inc., and now has 1,516 associates.

***Ogihara had (by early 1997) grown to 510 employees in Howell and had completed a metal stamping plant in Birmingham, Alabama, to supply major sheet metal panels to Mercedes-Benz. It was scheduled to employ 160 people when it reached full production in July 1997.

have tried to capture the sense of the group's experiences at each site. Many other features of the sites will be introduced in various places throughout the book. At this point, we want to set the stage for the analysis. The sites are introduced in chronological order according to the date of startup of production as a wholly owned or Japanese-affiliated company.

Hitachi Magnetics (1973)

Sixty miles north of Michigan State University is the small town of Edmore, Michigan, where Hitachi Magnetics purchased a plant from General Electric in the early 1970s. Despite the fact that the plant is located right in the town of Edmore, the site still feels rural. The farming community was, in fact, camouflage for what was originally a defense plant. Today the many small buildings of the Hitachi facility still blend into the landscape. However, reflections of the traditional management style that we use to describe Hitachi Magnetics are visible right away—in the parking spaces reserved for each executive and in the parking lot protected by barbed wire.

One of the few signs of interaction or involvement was the lobby display case, which contained quality awards and mementos of activities with the local schools and community. These displays were designed for visitors, not the employees. That is, the plant workers did not generally travel through the front lobby. In the office area, the furnishings were vintage gray, green, and brown metal reminiscent of the 1950s. We were struck by the small offices and the fact that the doors were closed, which seemed to symbolize the lack of opportunities for communication.

Once inside the plant, we were surprised to find that the manufacturing floor was congested and seemed jammed with machinery. The lighting was poor, and there was an array of banners encouraging safety and quality awareness. Workers wore no uniforms. As we toured the plant floor, we were led through a warren of small rooms and pockets of activity. This physical arrangement seemed to allow little opportunity for interaction among the workers, although there were a few flip charts near job sites for problem solving.

Due to the nature of the manufacturing operations, the plant contained a blast furnace that contributed to a hot and dirty atmosphere. Sand used for casting coated everything in that area. A dangerous aspect was the presence of highly volatile explosives in one or more rooms. In addition, we asked about one building that was completely shut off and were told that it was due for toxic cleanup and was resting on soil polluted by mercury.

The plant was subject to many pressures such as the residual pollution from the previous ownership, international competition, and the need for cost cutting. Both union and management had begun to recognize the need for change. They were trying to learn how to shift from the traditional adversarial labor–management relationship while also trying to move to a more efficient work organization system.

When the plant was purchased in 1973, the technology was state of the art, which was the most important factor for Hitachi Magnetics. Now, Hitachi Metal in Japan is a technological leader. The plant, meanwhile, has become less profitable over the years and has lost its technological edge. In an effort to improve operations, Hitachi Metal has begun to invest both capital and management expertise in the plant. Changes include attempts at reducing inventory, reducing health care costs, and infusing local management with Hitachi experts from European and Japanese operations.

Despite these changes, we still felt we were observing a traditional U.S. plant with little that reflected lean manufacturing practices. The site's layout presents a barrier to change in the work system. The Edmore facility also had an existing workforce. Workers were not selected or screened for the types of characteristics that the later Japanese-affiliated plants felt were essential for a new work culture.

Yamaha Musical Products (1973)

Yamaha Musical Products is in Grand Rapids, Michigan, just off 28th Street, one of the state's busiest stretches of road. The area is a mix of residential housing and suburban industrial buildings. The brown brick building is contemporary and modern looking with lots of dark, tinted glass. Visitors enter the facility via the reception area. The feel is businesslike, with sales and marketing offices just off the lobby. The office area is fairly open—several enclosed offices for functional area managers surround an open area for secretaries.

In the managers' offices the atmosphere was somewhat like an office furniture display area—very clean and functional. This businesslike area provided a backdrop for the close personal relationship that developed between two top managers—one Japanese and one American—who frequently stayed after everyone else had gone. They had many discussions about more than work issues. They spent hours talking about their families, cultures, and countries.

Despite this high-level relationship, there was very little that would tell others in the workforce that they were working for a Japanese company. For example, there were only a few Japanese managers and engineers. On the shop floor, the diversity was representative of the community, not of the ownership of the firm, including many Hispanic and Vietnamese women.

The manufacturing floor lay beyond two double doors in the office area. The contrast between the two areas was quite strong. On the manufacturing floor, the ceilings were high, the lighting was brighter, and the area was filled with workbenches. It was a large space reminiscent of a high school gymnasium.

At the workbenches, a number of operators, most of them women, added small parts to the instruments and then passed them to the next operators on small trays. This was the main activity. The atmosphere encouraged workers to do careful work: small cubicles separated workers from each other.

Each row of desks was a mini-assembly line without belts and conveyors—just small trays carried by hand from station to station. Finished instruments were passed into soundproof cubicles, where musicians were waiting to test each instrument. These musicians were hired for the acuity of their "ear"—a talent that could not be replicated by a machine.

Packers took each instrument and cleaned it carefully. Polished and glistening instruments were disassembled and packed into instrument cases, which were placed on small pallets and stored at the side in a vast storage area. (Core instruments or shells are shipped twice a year for sales spurts timed to match the beginning and end of the school year. A huge inventory of nonassembled parts must be kept on hand to prepare for this rush.)

Off to one side of the assembly area were separate rooms for percussion instrument parts assembly and final product assembly. We saw orchestra bells, timpani, and chimes. These pieces were all hand assembled in a form of craft assembly. There were two separate areas for special metal processing, one for buffing and polishing, and a clean room for lacquer and coating processes. These areas needed to remain dust free. The workers in these areas were paid a premium due to the nature of their work.

Although metal for instruments is finished here, the original bodies are made in Japan because the metal forming process is complex. Due to the significant investment and resulting economies of scale, we were told, it is cheaper to make them in Japan. Metal plating work is contracted out to other firms to avoid possible environmental impact and costs. In addition, instrument production is not a JIT process, so parts supply from Japan is feasible.

One surprise we had on our first visit to Yamaha was our chance meeting with the union bargaining chairman, who greeted and welcomed us and was obviously not surprised to see us. We had been concerned that all our contacts with this plant had been through management sources. We were scheduled to meet with the union on our next visit. Clearly, the management had let the union know about the research project—a possible sign of open communication on other matters as well.

We didn't see any meeting areas on the shop floor, though there were conference rooms in the plant. The company has a large cafeteria, with full vending facilities, that is used by both plant and office employees.

Above each work area were large lettered signs that identified the areas for tours. Students from local schools often toured the plant. Yamaha Corporation has a strong commitment to maintaining positive community relations. For example, the Yamaha Corporation funds an innovative program in which the Grand Rapids Symphony Orchestra is partnered with a class of third graders. The children listen to concerts for which they have selected the music.

Mazda (1983)/AAI (1992)

From the highway, the AAI plant looms huge and white in contrast to the flat landscape surrounding it. This is fitting, since AAI is a place of great contrasts. It is difficult to know which parts of the existing facility beyond the many chimneys are from its previous life as a Ford casting plant. Clearly, great attention has been paid to the details of the exterior and the lobby areas. The lobby is plush and open. Colors are rich. Models currently in production are on display among seating and meeting areas. Outside, the visitor sees areas of grass and large pieces of stone set up in an attractive design. The overall impression is strong, clean, and composed.

Once past the lobby, we were taken upstairs to an extensive conference room area, which was designed to allow a sense of great space; it even overlooked the lobby. The meeting rooms were modern and well appointed. The detail of space and design reflected a style of organization that fits with the theory of lean production. Each minute of our visit was scheduled, each location was planned and prepared, and the people strictly adhered to the plan.

When we had lunch in the cafeteria, the room was filled with noise, activity, and workers in their uniforms. Television monitors broadcast the latest news from production areas and other business-related information. In contrast, one wall was glass, through which a serene mini-garden was visible. Trees and carefully placed stones surrounded a small pond, creating a peaceful area. The surroundings and the choice of foods, both American and Japanese, made this one of the nicest cafeterias we visited.

Our structured visit continued as we left the cafeteria for a tour of the plant floor. The facilities were newer but at first glance very much like the production areas at NUMMI (discussed later). The cars moved through the building on a variety of assembly lines. "Doors-off" production allows components such as seats arriving at the specified time and place to be dropped immediately into the proper vehicle. This process was very impressive as it appeared seemingly effortless and clearly safer.

The plant was technologically the very picture of lean production. At that time, two models were being built on the same assembly line.[2] High levels of automation in areas like the body weld area, with its surreal atmosphere and strange music (signifying potential quality problems or actual line stoppage), also heightened our sense of a controlled environment. Lean production as we saw it at AAI was fast paced. The jobs appeared to demand constant effort and attention to details such as guards for belt buckles and covered fenders that prevented scratches and dings to the cars. Workers frequently appeared to be rushing to complete the tasks at their station. There were many group meeting areas, but they generally lacked personal touches—potted plants, posters, awards, announcements of birthdays, and holiday decorations—that we saw elsewhere.

One of the physical as well as emotional aspects of the alienation of the workers from the production system was the labor–management relationship. A portion of our team visited UAW Local 3000 at the union building a short drive from the plant site. While the union is proud of the product its members create, it is also wary of the production methods and philosophy driving the processes—an issue discussed in more detail in chapter 8.

NUMMI (1984)

Our first glimpse of NUMMI was a surprise. It is an older facility set among the low rolling hills of California near San Francisco. Leaving the highway, one drives past traditional factory fenced parking spaces and enters through a guard shack. From the lobby it is clear that the energies and resources of this plant go into less visible, more intangible factors such as the quality it is known for.

Our first stop was an upstairs office area surrounded by meeting rooms. The office area was completely open and filled with desks. We learned that the desks around the outside of the room belonged to higher-ranking NUMMI officials such as the plant manager while the center space was filled with people from a variety of different functional areas.

It was generally a functional space where people were working—either on their own or in small clusters. The atmosphere was relaxed and seemed informal.[3]

The factory floor reflected this same no-nonsense atmosphere. The lines were farther apart than at other lean facilities, but there was the same sense of efficiency and uncluttered functionality. Workers appeared less stressed than at AAI or Denso Manufacturing–Michigan, Inc., yet were obviously working hard. There was little inventory sitting about except what was needed at the moment. Similar to AAI, we saw "doors-off" production including the maze of conveyors that also moved car bodies and other components around the building. We watched workers bring new loads of parts to neatly organized racks or work stations.

Above the production area, there were electronic information boards. These boards had different colored lights and information displays. The different colored lights were used to show trouble status and location on the line; green indicates trouble-free operation, yellow means line slowdown, and red indicates line stoppage.

A problem developed and a red light blinked on immediately. People rushed to the trouble spot. Engineers, support personnel, line workers, and team leaders conferred and solved the problem within a very short time. Production resumed and the green light was re-lit. This we learned was the "andon board" described in various books on new work systems.

As we walked around the floor, we were surprised at the ease with which people were released from their tasks to talk with us and the amount of interaction there was between workers on the line. In addition, there were many meeting spaces where teams could sit and talk. The team areas were often filled with papers related to production and training as well as multicolored work process charts.

An odd symbol of the depth to which the Toyota management philosophy shapes events at NUMMI is an escalator, left over from the previous GM ownership, that is deliberately left dysfunctional. People walked up several long flights of steps to reach the cafeteria, and we admitted wishing the escalator worked. Management's decision to redirect the money needed to repair the escalator reflects the choices the company makes about what is important to the overall values and mission of the organization. It was an opportunity to reinforce symbolically the values of the organization. A functioning escalator doesn't improve quality, reduce waste, or add to customer satisfaction.

The principles of the organization were taken to a structural level when we visited the labor relations office. Members of the group were able to spend extended periods of time in this office to watch the activities that went on. This large open room was filled with desks arranged in pairs, with matched union and management representatives facing each other and sharing a telephone. When an issue arose—what might quickly become a written grievance in another setting—the union-management pair would investigate the facts. The environment was open and there was a constant buzz of conversation as people talked with each other and people across the room. There seemed to be little of the anger and hot language associated with the crisis and damage control that frequently exists in labor relations or union representatives' offices.

There was great diversity among the people in the plant—over 20 languages were spoken by the various groups of people working at NUMMI. The workers reflect the diversity of the San Francisco Bay Area. We saw little that indicated tensions among these many peoples, and we observed attention to details that signaled acceptance of diversity. For example, the food served in the cafeteria reflected a variety of cultural tastes: there was Japanese, Mexican, Italian, vegetarian, and Southeast Asian food. Unlike many facilities where uniforms were mandatory, NUMMI allows its workers to wear an eclectic blend of uniforms and other work clothes. We noticed that the company and union presidents, whom we met during our tour, were both wearing the same uniform.

Denso Manufacturing–Michigan, Inc. (1986)

The drive to Denso Manufacturing–Michigan, Inc., took us through rolling hills covered with trees on the outskirts of Battle Creek, Michigan. There were few other buildings. In fact, we had the sense that if the car broke down we'd have to walk miles to get help. This was one of the few industrial parks that actually looked like a park. The factory buildings didn't look like conventional manufacturing facilities. Orderliness characterized everything we saw and was apparent right at our approach. A well-landscaped lawn and recreational areas with tennis and basketball courts surrounded it. The entrance to the building seemed designed to draw visitors in toward the doors of the glass-walled lobby.

Once in the building, we passed through a modern and attractively laid-out lobby to the office areas. The office we saw was large and open—larger than a football field. People from all functional areas worked at desks that seemed really close together. Along the windows that formed one wall were desks for managers that faced inward. Throughout this space were meeting tables for small groups. Larger groups could meet in adjacent conference rooms. We were surprised that, while the president had his own conference room, his desk was out among the others in this office space.

The facility was new and clean. Everything seemed to be in its place for a reason. All employees had to use the card scanner when they entered and exited the building. In this area, we saw display cases containing visual safety records for each department, product samples, an onsite credit union with an ATM machine for employees (they are called associates), vending machines, and a cafeteria to one side. In the cafeteria, TV monitors and electronic message boards continuously updated associates about in-plant activities. Spaces were available for team activities like birthday parties. Interestingly, the displays containing EAP (Employee Assistance Program) brochures were in the bathrooms—reflecting appreciation for privacy and consideration for how best to communicate sensitive information.

We were told that almost $500,000 was spent on the construction and equipping of an in-house technical center. As we started out onto the plant floor, we also saw an area where robots were built and repaired.

The factory floor seemed orderly, compact, clean, well lit and ventilated, and quiet (considering the work going on). Machines were set close to each other in a flow-through manufacturing pattern. There was little vehicle traffic where the people were; small lots of parts were delivered by people using handcarts. At the ends of the lines, however, there was a beehive of activity as lift trucks loaded and unloaded materials for shipments every 20 to 30 minutes. Automation mixed with human effort in a high-tech environment.

Employees in this plant wore uniforms that included hats. Different colors indicated the status of the people wearing them. For example, team leaders had the same-colored hats as team members, and these hats contrasted with those worn by visitors.[4]

Team areas were highly visible and filled with charts, data sheets, and other work-related information. They were visibly functional areas where workers received and generated information about their production. Training materials and a training tracking system were posted at each area. Workers clearly were given large amounts of information and performance numbers on a regular basis. In some areas, we saw potted plants and family snapshots that added a more personal touch.

Ogihara (1986)

Just before you get off the expressway at the Howell, Michigan, exit, you can't miss the massive (and ever-expanding) white building on the north side of the road with the big blue letters announcing Ogihara. The plant site is centrally located amidst three automobile manufacturing centers—Lansing, Flint, and Detroit. It isn't clear what kind of business it is until you get into the plant. We learned that this family-owned business is primarily a die-making operation in Japan while it is a metal stamping business in this country. The plant supplies stamped pieces for several automobile companies. The product is very high-quality external metal components for vehicles like Ford's Continental, Town Car, Mark VI, and Probe.[5]

On the way to the facility, a visitor passes other factories, railroad tracks, and adjoining warehouse space. Outside the building, a fishing pond and picnic area maintain the peace of a rural atmosphere, and there is no gate or special parking outside the entrance.[6] The front reception area is simple; there is a modest waiting area and a display case filled with mementos and pictures of company-related events. Entry to all the main functional areas of the plant is possible off this reception area.

We were taken into a conference room across the hall from the president's office. This was a well-appointed room with comfortable chairs around a large table; it had pictures of the plant, maps recording the expansion of the buildings, and large, pressed metal auto body parts scattered about the corners. Clearly, the room was used for more than formal meetings and to entertain visitors. In fact, people left the room so we could use it, and then we were moved out to allow another group to meet. It was like the plant's family room.

Off the reception area was an office area that combined a large open space with smaller glass-walled offices for a few managers. (People use meeting areas in the office for consultation and discussion since this is a stamping plant with a high noise level.) Functional areas were clustered together in this space except for engineering, which had a large area upstairs above the main level.

Before we entered the factory floor, everyone had to put on hard hats, safety glasses, and earplugs. The plant was so clean and well laid out that these precautions seemed largely unnecessary. The space was enormous. It had high ceilings and overhead cranes that moved from one end of the plant to the other. The size of the room was necessary to accommodate the presses.

There were five press lines of varying size and length. Several of the presses were so big that we wondered how you could drop something the size of a small house and not shake the entire building. Press lines featured transfer equipment that moved the metal pieces from die to die automatically. Color-coded sets of massive dies were sitting next to the presses or in a storage area in the back of the plant. In addition, there were several areas that subassembled car body panels such as doors, deck lids, quarters, fenders, and roofs.

For a stamping plant, it was relatively quiet. The atmosphere hummed with activity, however. Forklifts were constantly moving materials from presses to staging areas. People at either end of the presses were monitoring press operations, loading the steel blanks, stacking the finished parts, and inspecting, as well as doing minor repairs on the parts. Despite the activity, the plant was so clean and orderly that one of our group members had no problem making the tour while she was on crutches.

The climate could be characterized as friendly and professional. We were frequently told about employees' experiences with the president of the company, who often walked through the plant and was known for his openness. In general, there seemed to be little tension between Americans and their Japanese colleagues. We heard many stories about social activities at work and outside of work. The Christmas parties were legendary: employees bring families and receive gifts from the company.

One area where people frequently interacted was the "awesome" cafeteria. Our group decided that this was our favorite cafeteria. We enjoyed the Japanese and American food as much as the employees. In fact, culinary arts were so important to this company that cafeteria support staff accompanied the Ogihara personnel who were sent to Mexico to consult on the Chrysler Neon project.

I/NTek (1990)

New Carlisle, the home of I/NTek, is located between South Bend and Michigan City, Indiana. The plant sits on a specially prepared site that looks deceptively like a cornfield. The large, white building is visible from a long way off due to the annealing tower that rises seven stories. We approached from the east, but the plant is connected directly with I-80 by access roads built to withstand the weight of the trucks moving steel in and out of the building. In addition, there is a railroad spur into the plant, which allows coils of steel to be unloaded at the back door.

The entrance to the plant was relatively simple. The reception area was functional, having a small seating area. Before the main office area was a corridor with small meeting rooms off to each side. We were taken to one of these small conference rooms to interview the human resource manager. This little room was our home base during our entire visit except for a plant tour.

As we walked out to the plant floor, there was a gradual transition to a manufacturing environment. The people we began to meet wore hard hats and steel-toed boots. Soon everyone was wearing hard hats, which we learned were color-coded to indicate the wearer's status in the plant. Ours were white for visitors.

We were taken through the plant to the dock area where the steel coils come into the plant off the railroad cars. At this point the steel coils begin the rolling process. As one coil ends, another is welded to it. This is an amazing and crucial point in the process since the plant operates continuously. Next, the steel goes through scaling tanks where the surface is cleaned of rust. The scaling area is specially designed to protect the area's ground water from pollution due to the chemicals used in the process. The interior of the building is dark and rusty colored—matching this process.

Our tour took us up stairs and along catwalks over the equipment, then down again nearer the machinery. The roller repair area is a large space, perhaps the size of a baseball infield, devoted to grinding and polishing the rollers. Seven miles of rollers guide and flatten the steel as it coils through the plant. The equipment makes handling the steel look easy. It seems thin and malleable, yet the tension of the metal hangs in the air because it is potentially so dangerous. Operators can stop the line when they feel there are quality or safety issues at stake. When the mill stops for longer than a few minutes, the steel must be rethreaded through the system, which can take up to three days. At different places along the process, two or three minutes of slack are built in to allow adjustments or roller changes.

We did not see many people at work in the rolling mill. Most workers monitor the process from control rooms. It seemed that control and monitoring were the chief duties of the people in the plant. We assumed that charts and other pieces of information not available on the computer were also kept in these areas since we saw little of that material on the floor. It is possible that the danger inherent in this environment kept people off the floor except when necessary. Protective clothing made it difficult to judge the diversity of the workforce, although we did see some women.

There were a few more people in the coating section of the building, known as I/N Kote.[7] At the time of our visit this was a new section. It looks like a giant model of a futuristic city. The machinery is multilayered and has rows of different-colored lights. The cold-rolled steel enters this equipment and winds like ribbon candy through it to a central point where it flashes through a zinc bath and goes straight up for seven stories. The silver ribbon of steel comes immediately back down as it cools and then enters another section of equipment.

As the cooled metal comes out of the galvanizing process, it is coiled onto a spool. This process is also continuous so that special machinery allows one coil to end as another starts. The coils are wrapped and banded and moved on an automated transport vehicle (ATV). The ATVs, which are named after the Seven Dwarfs, take the coils to a multistory storage area. The storage area is computer controlled; once again, there didn't appear to be many people involved in the process.

Coil Center (1991)

The Coil Center is just off the expressway near Howell, Michigan. The building is not visible from the highway and appears to be a big warehouse. This is the smallest of the sites we visited. The reception area has just a few seats and an adjacent office space. The American and Japanese senior executives have offices connected by doors—just to the right of the front door. Standing here, one can see the glass wall that separates the office area (with its closely packed desk cubicles) from the factory (with its high ceiling, large equipment, and inventory of unused steel rolls or finished stampings).

This reinforced glass wall is sprinkled with notices and information charts related to the production activities. The glass is 6 to 8 feet high and perhaps 20 feet wide. The glass runs the length of the reception area. The wall separates two different worlds, the business world of secretaries and sales people from the noisier blue-collar zone. The two worlds watch each other through this wall, almost creating jealousy between them. There seemed to be a perception that management people spent a disproportionate amount of time in the office world.

The building houses one huge press line for blanking. The work area also feels like two worlds, one that surrounds the press line and one that is concerned with banding and shipping the steel blanks. There are perhaps 15 to 20 employees on the floor during the day shift. The afternoon shift is a bit smaller and much more relaxed. Workers in the afternoon shift feel less stressed, which might be due to the absence of managers, interruptions, and visitors. Workers on this second shift were able to be less formal (they even bring gas grills to work from time to time to prepare community meals).

The building is bright and clean. The equipment is colorful and new. Big rolls of coiled steel sit ready to run through the press. Workers are assigned to stations, and most activity occurs when the coils need to be changed. The shipping area seems busier, perhaps due to the work. It isn't a true JIT supplier since parts are often produced in advance. A week or two of each customer's parts are stored in the building; this stockpile creates a buffer in case of changes or equipment problems. The company tries to keep the one press in operation continuously during the two shifts. Time between the shifts is used for preventive maintenance.

There is a small kitchen or coffee area big enough for a small group to sit and eat. It is very informal and would not be big enough for the entire group of employees to meet at one time. The only space big enough for this type of meeting is the plant floor where the press runs. There is a small resource room where employees can refer to the manuals and training guides used during the startup.

For a small new facility, this company had a number of different worlds: the office and floor, the regulars and the temporaries, the first and second shifts, and the original employees and the next generation hired. The fax machine also created a cultural gap when the daily reports were sent off in Japanese to the head offices of Tomen. This one site was a microcosm of some of the differences we saw elsewhere.

Conclusion

We began this chapter with the simple observation that the physical setting in which we work matters. It is important to note, however, that the meaning of the physical workplace varies across companies, regions, and even national cultures. For many U.S. workers, for example, the workplace merely represents the location in which labor is exchanged for pay. There may be informal communities that exist among co-workers, but this broader social meaning is often seen as incidental or even contrary to the business operation. In contrast, there is a much stronger assumption in most Japanese workplaces that the worker is part of the shared community. As such, the expectation is that workers—as responsible citizens—will contribute to a clean, safe working environment.

Attention to the physical setting was highlighted for us by a Japanese expression that appeared in various forms in a number of our sites. While we are still learning about the full cultural meaning of the expression, we encountered in our sites various versions of a Japanese expression that roughly translates as "the five S's."

In Japanese, these five S's are *Seiri, Seiton, Seiso, Seiketsu,* and *Shitsuke.* Seiri refers to determining the essentials or sorting out the unnecessary. Seiton stands for ordering these essentials or putting things in the proper place. Seiso is for cleaning, as in sweeping the floor. Seiketsu stands for cleanliness, including personal hygiene. Shitsuke refers to the discipline to maintain the practices, including doing tasks the same way every time.[8] Incorporating these five concepts into work practices is a key element of most Japanese production systems—even if it is often overlooked.

At one level, these five S's describe an approach toward the physical space that calls for a much higher level of individual care, attention, and responsibility than is typically expected of most U.S. workers. In this respect, it is a reminder to keep machines clean, to avoid clutter on the floor, and other such behaviors. At a deeper level, the five S's are the building blocks that create the ability to consistently perform the basic tasks of production well. They represent a mindset that focuses energy on strategically important tasks such as reducing waste, increasing flexibility, and preventing disruption or unexpected down time.

It is immediately apparent when you enter a workplace in which these ideas are built into the culture. There is an absence of clutter and an apparent orderliness or logic to what may even be highly frenetic activities. We saw this in many of our U.S. sites and then had the image reinforced even more strongly when we visited the parent factories in Japan. There are, of course, some U.S. locations with no apparent links to Japan where the same attention to space can be found. These are often places where there is a strong, shared workplace culture and a high degree of pride.

We suspect that the five S's represent a powerful vehicle for ordering thinking in ways that support effective workplace operations. In the absence of these principles, the same workplace effort is less likely to yield the same results—since it will be less focused or channeled and will be impaired by clutter or unplanned events. The concepts may begin on the shop floor, but it has important implications at other levels. We suspect that the concepts may show up in the work practices of middle managers, engineers, union leaders, and others who work in settings that have these physical characteristics. We know from some of the workers we met that the practices are certainly carrying over into their home lives. In this sense, the physical workplace and the approach to it shapes thinking in ways that can have far-reaching implications.

We have reviewed the physical attributes of our research sites not just to create a mental picture of these settings. We hope we have begun to convey an understanding of the many ways in which these physical settings serve as a context for new work practices.

3

Cross-Cultural Diffusion

· ·

S uccess in a global economy requires mastery of the diffusion of
innovation. Diffusion of knowledge-driven work systems is increasingly a primary source of competitive advantage for business. Its importance equals such traditional sources of competitive advantage as capital,
technology, and geography. New production techniques and work organization systems are central to the dramatic gains that can be achieved
in quality and productivity. Clearly, companies, unions, workers, and
societies must understand the implications of these new work practices
as well as the processes by which they are diffused.

The diffusion of work practices may begin with an organization
deciding to establish operations in another location.[1] Such a decision is
deceptively easy to announce, and many people do not have a genuine
understanding of what is a most complex process. At the heart of the
process are strategic choices regarding how to set up the work system in
the new location.

Establishment of a new work system can be attempted primarily
through imposition of a complete system, it can emerge out of extensive interactions, or it can unfold in other ways. Further, there are subtle,
intangible elements of the process that end up having dramatic implications in the ultimate outcome. Our discussion will describe how the
intangible and tangible elements of the diffusion process combine with
the interactions of people to create knowledge.

The Japanese–U.S. Case

Cross-cultural diffusion has been observed since the rise of recorded
history. Work practices and skills traveled over early trade routes along

36

with people and commodities. Scholars have documented the value of skills and knowledge in the ancient guild system or the arrival of Westerners in Japan.[2] This book focuses on one of the most recent parts of this ongoing story, the co-evolution of U.S. and Japanese industry.[3]

Representatives from Japanese industry visited post–World War II U.S. companies to see what made them the most successful mass producers in the world. Exact duplication of this system was not possible in the Japanese context at that time.[4] For example, since usable land was so limited, the inventory storage methods used in the United States were not feasible. Similarly, the establishment of new facilities by vertically integrated trading companies in Japan facilitated the location of suppliers close to assembly operations. Through a process of selection and adaptation, a variant on the U.S. mass production system began to dominate manufacturing in Japan. The characteristics of this system have been well described by others, with features such as JIT delivery, reduced in-process inventory, and SPC.[5] While the characteristics are well documented, the process by which they are transferred to the United States is less familiar. We will describe how work system components have been returning in the form of quality and production management systems since the 1970s.

In the United States, the oil crisis and increased imports from Japan forced American manufacturers to recognize a new source of competitive advantage. When it became apparent that firms needed to change to compete, each organization started at a different place and proceeded through a unique set of steps. These changes are all part of a diffusion process that is important, complex, and often little understood.

Dynamics over Time

Capital investment is not in itself usually associated with diffusion of work practices.[6] The first major wave of manufacturing investment in the 1970s made little or no attempt to transfer contemporary Japanese management or production practices.[7] The diffusion story begins in what we are calling the second wave of Japanese investment in the United States. In table 3.1, we categorize the companies we visited by four characteristics: type of production technology, ownership status, wave of Japanese investment, and type of team system.

As the second wave of Japanese investment arrived in the United States, the dynamics of global competition and a global economy drove an evaluation of strategic business practices. United States firms were no longer unchallenged leaders in many markets. In the 1980s, Japa-

Table 3.1   Team Type at Research Sites Classified by Production Technology, Timing of Japanese Investment, and Ownership Status

Timing of Japanese Investment	Ownership Status	Production Technology		
		Continuous Production	Batch Production	Assembly
First Wave of Investment (pre-1980)	Joint Venture Japanese Subsidiary		Hitachi Magnetics Corp. *Off Line Teams*	Yamaha Musical Products *Off Line Teams*
Second Wave of Investment (post-1980)	Joint Venture	I/NTek (Inland/Nippon) *STS Teams*	Coil Center (Tomen/Kasle) *STS Teams*	AAI (Mazda/Ford) *Lean Teams* NUMMI (Toyota/GM) *Lean Teams*
	Japanese Subsidiary		Ogihara Corporation *Lean Teams*	Denso Manufacturing–Michigan, Inc. *Lean Teams*

Adapted from Work Practices Diffusion Team "Japanese Team-Based Work Systems in the United States: Explaining the Diversity," *California Management Review* 47 (1994): 53.

nese companies invested more than money in the American marketplace. They also brought their work organization systems and introduced them to U.S. workers, managers, and union leaders.

A key question centers on why the Japanese waited until the 1980s to export a successful production system. They may have feared that some practices were inherently "Japanese" and could not be accepted or implemented effectively by non-Japanese workers.[8] Despite increasing success in global markets, Japanese companies took some time to gain confidence in the new practices. But these companies were encouraged to introduce a more effective work system by pressures such as a doubling of U.S. market share, demands for quality, currency fluctuations, a desire on the part of these companies to be close to their customers, and threatened trade tariffs. Furthermore, diffusion is at least a two-way process, and American manufacturers were not ready to accept what has come to be termed lean production because of their belief in the superiority of U.S. manufacturing. Finally, competition between Japanese companies drove the export of work systems as well as products. For all of these reasons, a number of Japanese firms adopted the goal of producing the same high-quality, low-cost products that were made in Japan, but in a U.S. setting.

At first, Americans noticed the results achieved by Japanese companies that used what we are calling knowledge-driven production, but the Americans were not clear about the processes by which they were achieved. Gaps in productivity and quality frequently led U.S. firms to the piecemeal introduction of innovative practices. Firms tried quality circles, JIT delivery, SPC, teams, or suggestion programs. For the most part, they did not fully understand that these individual programs were interdependent within an entire system. As we now know, the practices produced vastly different results when taken out of context. Quality circles, for example, became gripe sessions rather than an element of process improvement. It is now clear that lean production requires more than an assortment of individual components. It requires a highly integrated system that can be flexible enough to allow for a type of individualized adaptation across firms.

A Close Look at the First Wave

The first-wave locations initially faced a competitive environment based on the traditional mass production system. These facilities were often able to succeed in a mass production environment without a dedicated supplier network or concepts of employment security. In addition, they were more accountable to domestic economic pressures than to the forces of the international marketplace.

The two oldest sites in our study, Yamaha Musical Products and Hitachi Magnetics, are examples of the first wave of investment. Both feature relatively traditional forms of work organization. When these sites first came under Japanese ownership, there were no attempts to change to the work system utilized in Japanese plants owned by the same companies.

Hitachi Metals bought the plant from General Electric (GE), continued relations with the United Auto Workers (UAW), and maintained the traditional, legalistic approach to collective bargaining. The focus of Hitachi Metals' investment initially was to acquire GE's technology and add capacity for the production of magnets. In the case of Yamaha Musical Products, the company established production with a focus on final assembly of instruments for sale in the United States.

Today, a shift is occurring at both locations. In the early 1990s, each company began introducing selected Japanese work practices. For example, at Hitachi Magnetics, groups of employees are utilized as "off-line" teams for weekly problem-solving meetings. Off-line teams are a modern form of quality circles that closely resemble improvement efforts at many unionized U.S. firms. Although these teams do not represent a complete reorganization of production around a team system, they do reflect an increased level of involvement by the Japanese parent in work practices at its U.S. site.

We see this as evidence that the first wave of Japanese investment in North America did not represent the influx of Japanese work practices that received so much attention in the business press. Instead, these facilities added manufacturing capacity while using local employment-relations practices, most of which are still in place. This finding directly challenges any unitary view of Japanese investment in North America.

There are many possible explanations why Japanese-owned firms maintained traditional North American employment-relations practices. Where existing facilities were purchased, such as Hitachi Magnetics in Edmore, many practices were firmly established and were hard to change. At Hitachi and at Yamaha Musical Products, the workers were represented by the UAW, and collective bargaining agreements had instilled a range of standard expectations about work rules, wages, and benefits. Underlying these explanations, however, is a deeper issue. Japanese executives in our sites indicated that the Japanese firms were not as confident in the 1970s as they are now regarding the merits of their work systems. Also, U.S. consultants firmly advised companies to maintain "local" practices.

A Close Look at the Second Wave

After 1980, in what we call the second wave of investment, Japanese practices changed. The change began with some high-profile, explicit, and comprehensive efforts to import or develop new systems of work practices. Two examples of this type of effort are NUMMI and AAI.[9] At other newly constructed locations such as Coil Center and Denso Manufacturing–Michigan, Inc., local consultants and U.S. managers were still hired for advice on best local practice, but the firms also brought their own views on how to run manufacturing operations. Thus, the timing of the Japanese investment is a key factor in explaining the presence or absence of work practice diffusion.

The increased ability of suppliers to produce high-quality and low-cost parts in a timely manner is a further element of the successful transfer of Japanese production to the United States. Traditional mass production–based American firms could not meet these standards quickly enough in most cases. In the auto industry, Japanese assemblers were compelled to bring their suppliers with them or continue shipping parts from home. Eventually, as U.S. trade rules stiffened, Japanese firms began to share information and procedures with American suppliers to help them improve their internal operations. New types of producer-supplier relationships developed over time. The successes of their work organization systems began to convince traditional producers to experiment and learn how to compete in this new environment.

Davis Jenkins tested our hypothesis about two waves of investment with Florida and Kenney's sample of 229 Japanese-affiliated auto supply plants in the United States.[10] Jenkins confirmed the preliminary case evidence of two distinct sets of work practices (Jenkins's paper is an excellent example of linking grounded research to subsequent hypothesis testing). More work is still to be done on this issue, however. For example, there is some evidence that more traditional work systems still exist in electronics factories built in North America in the mid- and late 1980s.[11] It would be important to know how these factories compare to those producing similar products in Japan and whether the level of confidence in production technology in this sector is comparable to that in the automotive, auto supply, and steel sectors. Ultimately, these findings have strategic implications that reach far beyond the specific case of Japanese investment in North America.[12]

The Japanese parent companies of the facilities we visited faced a core strategic decision about the best way to invest internationally. It is hard to find public statements on whether their goal at the time was just to add productive capacity while retaining local work practices or to transplant "best in class" work practices in the new operations. Clearly, however, the latter strategy holds the greatest promise for sustained competitive advantage. But this strategy also involves the complex challenge of identifying the most promising mix of work practices in the home and host countries. All of our second-wave sites feature such combinations of work practices (illustrating co-evolution). As we will see in the following section, the second wave of Japanese investment has stimulated learning across major segments of both American and Japanese industry.

Embedded in this story is the shift from the mass production model to a knowledge-driven model that may well be setting the stage for work systems in the next century. Indeed, the knowledge-driven nature of the work systems exported with the second wave of Japanese investment has a dynamic quality. The learning process itself serves to reinforce and extend the cross-cultural exchange.

Toward a Theory of Work Practice Diffusion

The concept of diffusion has roots in the many disciplines and literatures concerned with technology, innovation, and culture. Diffusion is often described in ways that highlight the end result but are not fully attentive to the dynamic nature of the process. For example, scholars will observe innovations or cultural patterns in two different settings and examine what is similar or different between them—they focus on these "end results." This approach leads to an emphasis on the diffusion of products or other easily observable characteristics.

In this context, diffusion is usually defined in mechanistic terms. For example, Rogers's classic analysis of diffusion highlights four elements: the innovation, the channels of communication, time, and the social system.[13] Most models of diffusion take as their point of departure the source or sender. We believe diffusion begins not with the sender but with what Rogers terms the adopter. It is only at the point that people take up an innovation that diffusion occurs.

Diffusion is shaped by the original intent of the sending party. However, the intent cannot be fully understood except in retrospect, based on the multilevel interactions between the sender and the adopter. In this sense, diffusion can be said to be occurring only when interactions have begun. In building a more dynamic and interactive approach to diffusion, we will use some of the concepts and ideas that Rogers and others have introduced, but we will also be introducing some new concepts that we have developed to help organize our thinking about what we observed. The new ideas are organized around what might be termed the structure, strategy, and processes for diffusion.

The Structure for Diffusion

As we begin to construct a framework for understanding the diffusion of work practices, we must first identify the structure within which interactions occur. We identify three main modes of diffusion: primary, secondary, and reverse. Each mode represents a classification of the direction in which diffusion is initiated.

Primary diffusion consists of the original movement of ideas from a source to a receiver through a given channel. While these ideas or practices are likely to have deeper roots, there is an ostensibly clear source and receiver. The extension of the Toyota production system from the Takaoka plant in Japan to the NUMMI joint venture in California would be an example of primary diffusion.

In the Takaoka–NUMMI case, consider the Toyota system's core principle that the shop-floor workers are regarded as the most important internal customers of everyone else in the organization. The primary diffusion of this concept, perhaps more than any other, is responsible for the emergence of constructive and effective relations at NUMMI. Under GM management, the workforce and union leadership had been known as some of the most contentious in the GM system and had a record of poor quality and high costs. Note that it is not just the diffusion of the technical, tangible aspects of the Takaoka plant that we are considering but also the diffusion of intangible factors and principles such as the concept of kaizen.

Secondary diffusion involves movement from a receiver to a further set of receivers. Here the recipient in primary diffusion seeks to extend these ideas to others. The efforts by NUMMI to educate its suppliers regarding the Toyota production system are an example of secondary diffusion. Similarly, at AAI the UAW local learned principles from the Japanese managers and engineers that helped them organize the workers at four of AAI's suppliers. The knowledge and processes being diffused in these cases of secondary diffusion will have been modified from the original ideas or practices. These are not one-time events; secondary diffusion, like primary diffusion, is a process of co-evolution.

This points to the third structure, reverse diffusion. Reverse diffusion involves the flow of ideas from a receiver back to a source. It can occur in either the primary or secondary situations. This activity occurs in many stages. In the first stage, information passes from one person, unit, company, or culture to another and is modified through integration into the existing knowledge base. This new, shared knowledge is then transferred back to the original sender. For example, Dr. Deming's ideas traveled to Japan, became integrated into a shared base of knowledge within Japanese firms, and are now returning to the United States. Further, U.S. changes in these innovations are now finding their way back to parent firms in Japan, extending what is a potentially endless cycle.

When we were in Japan and meeting with representatives from Toyota at the Takaoka plant, a U.S. scholar (on the same tour with us) asked a series of questions about specific practices that had been adopted at Toyota's new Kyushu plant. The questions were asked with the implication that mistakes had been made in the past and adjusted in this new facility. The responses were ambiguous—either it was difficult for these managers to see themselves as part of a reverse diffusion process or they did not want to discuss sensitive internal issues.

A member of our team asked a similar question but in a very different way. He noted that Toyota's materials indicate that the Corolla is made in fourteen companies and fourteen different countries as well as in the Takaoka plant. In this context, he asked if they have ever taken information or ideas from the other plants and used them at the Takaoka plant. Instantly, there was intense interest, extensive dialogue, and numerous examples concerning the issue. The production manager of the plant pointed to the frequency of job rotation at NUMMI (where he had recently worked). At NUMMI, rotation occurs twice a day for ergonomic reasons; at Takaoka it occurs every six months (if at all). He said that this idea was brought back to Takaoka, where it was then adopted. Stated in this way, the concept of reverse diffusion was both understandable and seen as important. The experience also reveals the importance and difficulty of taking a non-blaming, constructive approach to issues of knowledge and diffusion.

Managers, union leaders, engineers, workers, and others are often unprepared for reverse diffusion. Senders do not expect the receivers to send new or reformulated ideas back. Managers from another Japanese facility that we visited explicitly stated that they were the experts and had nothing to learn from other countries making similar products. Yet this feedback loop may be the most important part of the diffusion process.

The cross-cultural dynamics of diffusion were clearly illustrated by the experiences of one Japanese manager whom we interviewed in Japan, after a multiyear assignment in the United States. He indicated that he had learned a valuable management lesson from his American counterpart, which involved the use of positive reinforcement. He explained that managers in Japan use more negative than positive reinforcement. As it happens, the negative reinforcement in Japan is non-blaming, which is in contrast with negative reinforcement that is commonly given in the United States. After observing the increased use of positive reinforcement in the United States, this manager reported that he too found himself using it more often. Back in Japan, he indicated that he continued to use more positive reinforcement with Japanese workers and he found it very effective.

From other returnees we heard similar stories around their increased use of positive reinforcement after returning to Japan. Thus, the primary diffusion involves Japanese managers assigned to the United States to help implement a new manufacturing system. The reverse diffusion involves an adjustment in how to best manage in the context of that system. We would anticipate, however, that the concept of positive reinforcement will be adapted if it diffuses in the Japanese context. A true measure of whether reverse diffusion had taken place might be if a next generation of Japanese managers brought these adapted approaches to positive reinforcement with them when they came on assignment to U.S. operations.

All three diffusion structures have distinct intended outcomes. Senders are introducing work practices for specific reasons and expect concrete results. Unforeseen aspects of diffusion lead inevitably, however, to unintended consequences. These frequently develop as a receiver responds to new ideas. These serendipitous responses often prove to be more robust than the original ideas because they are shaped by the experiences and knowledge of the individuals or groups who work with them.

Strategies for Diffusion

The diffusion structures—primary, secondary, and reverse—help to classify the direction of the flow of ideas. However, a closer look at the process of diffusion quickly moves beyond this simple framework. In any workplace, change occurs through formal as well as informal channels. Informal channels may be more difficult to identify, but the change strategies can be inferred by examining how the ideas are introduced. We observed three major strategies for the introduction of work practices and have termed them piecemeal, imposed, and negotiated.

In some cases, the introduction occurs on a piecemeal basis when ideas from Japan are introduced as isolated or separate components taken out of the context of the entire system. Here various practices are added to an existing work system in an ad hoc way. Hitachi Magnetics initially adopted the existing General Electric mass production technology, union contract, and work system. Over time, plant management at Edmore has tried to improve production processes by the introduction of individual practices. For example, Hitachi introduced the concept of SPC charting in the early 1990s. This was a special initiative rather than an embedded component of a fundamentally different work system. The piecemeal approach is possible in the context of a more traditional mass production work system. Because of the many buffers built into such a system, piecemeal experimentation with new practices will not necessarily disrupt operations.

In other cases, a new work system is an imposed strategy: an intact model of an existing work system is transferred to a new location and workforce. Some Japanese companies tried to export a successful production system to the United States without fully understanding the implications or the obstacles resulting from legal and cultural constraints. For example, Mazda's assembly operation in Hiroshima was a well-developed model of production and was used as a blueprint for the AAI operations in Flat Rock. The intent seems to have been to fully replicate the social and technical features of their existing system. Difficulties may have developed in part because, while technology could be transferred, human resource systems such as compensation or training were of necessity much different. There was also little or no initial input from the people receiving the work system, which allowed assumptions and expectations among all involved to go unchecked.[14]

A third set of cases features interactions that fit neither the piecemeal category nor the imposed introduction category. An integrated and highly successful work system may be in place in the home country—in this case, Japan—but the firm takes what we have termed a negotiated approach. The intent is to construct a system using the input of the workforce and other experts within the constraints imposed by the company's overall plan and the unique conditions at the new location.

This reflects a clear expectation that the resulting work system will be neither a set of separately added pieces nor a re-creation of an existing system. Instead, it is anticipated that it will be the product of a variety of formal and informal negotiation processes at all levels of the organization. For example, at Denso Manufacturing–Michigan, Inc., and Ogihara, the startup phase featured extensive dialogue and debate among Japanese and U.S. employees regarding the practices to be utilized. More specifically, while Japanese managers may have been very clear in their insistence on the principle of in-station quality inspection, the specific ways in which this was accomplished were adapted through negotiation to the U.S. context.

By "negotiation," we are not just referring to formal collective bargaining with its designated sides and explicit give-and-take. We are also referring to informal interactions in which practices are considered, debated, tested, and incorporated into people's daily routines. This is a continuous process that occurs in ways that are not always perceived as negotiation. For example, team members at Denso Manufacturing–Michigan, Inc., are encouraged to coordinate proposed changes in their work area with internal "customers'" downstream and internal "suppliers'" upstream from them. These conversations on the subject of changes are, in fact, a form of negotiation.

Neither the lean production system nor the STS knowledge-driven work system can be diffused on a piecemeal basis, yet that is exactly what many organizations attempt to do. They conduct "benchmarking" visits and pick selected tangible features of the operation to adopt. A particular team size may be selected, a specific rotation policy might be chosen, or a suggestion program may be implemented. Insufficient consideration is given to the context from which this single item is drawn, and the intangible elements that support it may not be immediately available in the new setting. Elements of any knowledge-driven system are most difficult to transfer as single items, and success is usually limited at best. This type of attempt more typically ends in failure.

Far more complicated, however, is the choice between an imposed and a negotiated strategy for diffusion. Many managers are drawn to the imposed model: it promises concrete changes that are (or are not) accepted in a relatively tight time frame. However, the imposed approach is only seemingly easier. For example, at NUMMI many features of the Toyota production system were initially imposed. This was later modified, and the parties now appear to have shifted to a negotiated diffusion strategy.

The imposed approach is limited in the way it concentrates energy on tangible elements of each component of the system. It also can directly undercut some of the intangible elements of team-based work—for example, trust and constructive working relations.

The negotiated approach is the most ambiguous. Clearly, there are some underlying principles that are either not negotiable or subject only to minor adjustment. The principle of kaizen, for example, may not be negotiable even if the particular systems to foster continuous improvement are. To effectively implement a negotiated strategy for diffusion, parties need to be very knowledgeable about the work systems as well as the workplace environment into which they will be transferred. It is also crucial for the parties to be committed to a long-term learning process since, even with the best of knowledge, unanticipated consequences emerge.

These three diffusion strategies—piecemeal, imposed, and negotiated—are ideal types. The actual experience in each case was and is not a pure type. Also, and more important, we observed changes in the strategies over time in some of the organizations we studied.

The Diffusion Process

We began defining diffusion with traditional structural definitions involving receivers (or adopters) and senders. We added a structural dimension involving the direction of diffusion, including primary, secondary, and reverse diffusion. To this still partial definition, we added strategies for the introduction of an innovation—piecemeal, imposed, and negotiated. To complete the framework, we will now introduce knowledge creation as the ultimate process by which diffusion occurs.

All workplaces possess the ingredients for knowledge creation: people, information, and mechanisms to create knowledge. There are, however, dramatic differences in how these essential components are viewed and deployed, and these differences affect the knowledge-creation process as well as the relationships among elements of the workplace. When workers combine their individual knowledge and shared experience to work out a solution to a problem or workplace dilemma, virtual knowledge is created as part of the process. What happens next is the key to using this potent force.

As new and exciting knowledge is directed into solutions for workplace dilemmas, it changes into explicit knowledge. It becomes "the new way we do things." Virtual knowledge has limited value in itself. Yet the emergent, shared understandings can become a powerful foundation for action, improvement, and continued learning. The quality of the knowledge-creation process depends directly, of course, on the quality and interaction of inputs. Diverse perspectives serve to enrich the options considered and the applicability of the knowledge generated.

Ideas travel through a structure and are guided by a strategy, but diffusion will occur only to the degree the individuals adjust their thinking or behavior. These shifts don't just happen. They are preceded by the knowledge-creation process, which we suggest begins with the creation of virtual knowledge. It is often impossible to pinpoint the beginnings of such creation processes.

In our work, one of the starting points was foreign investment by Japanese firms. Investment by these firms takes the form of capital, work practices, or entire production systems. When these tangible elements are combined with a mechanism that encourages interaction among workers in a group, virtual knowledge is one very fundamental outcome. We know from observing its creation that virtual knowledge is fragile. This leads to this book's central irony, which is that the vast global process of work practice diffusion depends on something as fragile as virtual knowledge.

Competency-Based Diffusion

We have described the diffusion structures and strategies that we observed during our research. However, for the practical reader the important point here is how these systems are implemented and what helps them to be successful. As we said earlier, beyond the dynamics of the initial introduction process we are interested in the continuous adoption of innovation. We will take a closer look at the impact of the introduction strategy at each of the locations we visited.

Despite great variation in the details at each location, patterns stand out. Although we realize that each case of diffusion is unique, we will highlight these patterns because of their importance to those engaged in the transfer of technology and information.

Two of our sites, Hitachi Magnetics and Yamaha Musical Products, illustrate the problems that can develop as firms introduce innovative practices in piecemeal fashion. Each was a successful company when they were acquired by their Japanese parent firm. These sites were purchased in an era when mass production was the dominant mode. Organizational communication came down from the top of the hierarchy, while labor and employment relations followed the dominant patterns of the era. For example, the relationship with the UAW local was wary, and collective bargaining was a predictable adversarial process.

By the time we visited these locations, the pressures of competition were pushing them to experiment and introduce elements of other production systems. No attempt was made to introduce an entire new production system to either facility. For example, a senior manager at Hitachi described the introduction of the concept of kaizen as follows: "Kaizen was brought in by the Japanese, but it has been a 'cut and paste' process." The introduction of even a few new elements met with resistance from existing interests such as the workforce, management, union, and product constraints.

To reconcile the divergent forces involved in such changes, both firms will likely have to move toward more negotiated modes of interaction. This stage has formal and informal types of negotiation, although the formal collective bargaining sessions are still concerned with issues such as job classifications rather than with developing rules for team-based systems.

Two cases, NUMMI and Ogihara, were initially labeled imposed introductions. In both instances, the Japanese affiliate firms had well-designed, effective work organization systems that were in part responsible for their success. When the decision was made to move operations to this country, it was a logical choice to transfer a system known to be effective. Efforts to move an intact work organization system were initially successful, but in both cases the strains of a cross-cultural, international move caused the firms to shift to a more negotiated approach. The imposed approach was abandoned because it was unrealistic to try to bring every detail of a system to a new country. The knowledge-driven nature of the work systems mandated mechanisms that encouraged discussion and learning. These negotiation mechanisms helped to create a more functional set of procedures.

At AAI, the shift was dramatic. The initial imposed strategy dissolved into a more piecemeal approach. We believe that the intangible elements in a relationship were the pivotal factors in this shift. Early in the AAI startup period, the firm tried to introduce the entire Mazda production system to the workers at the Flat Rock plant. Among the important elements that shaped startup activities were the existing relationship between Ford and the UAW, state government intervention, and special local government initiatives.[15] When the tangible elements of the work system were put in place, workers received training in the important parts of the program.[16] This training highlighted both tangible and intangible elements of the production system.

Unfortunately, neither the Japanese executives nor the American workforce fully attended to underlying differences in cultural assumptions—especially about fairness.[17] When incidents triggered adverse reaction among the workers, management did not understand what had happened. For example, the existence of a written contract raises two separate sets of expectations among Americans and Japanese. Americans are more likely to expect a literal and legalistic interpretation, while the Japanese are more likely to view a contract as guidelines to be used as appropriate in a given situation.[18] Such misunderstandings were difficult to reconcile, and the transfer of elements of the work system was affected. The diffusion process shifted to a piecemeal strategy. This represented the only alternative when the imposed approach failed and the negotiated approach met resistance.

The experience across these three sites suggests that an initial imposed strategy is ineffective for the cross-cultural diffusion of work practices. Insistence on imposing a highly specific set of interconnected practices will either evolve into a negotiated new system or disintegrate into piecemeal implementation efforts.

Finally, there is some evidence to suggest that two of our locations, I/NTek and Denso Manufacturing–Michigan, Inc., began with a negotiated approach from the outset. Even though both of the Japanese parent organizations had well-established and successful production systems, neither insisted on the wholesale transfer of these systems. In the case of I/NTek, both the union and the U.S. managerial team prompted extensive dialogue and shared construction of the new work system. At Denso Manufacturing–Michigan, Inc., it was really a corporate philoso-

phy and culture, with the help of key local managers, that set the stage
to anticipate knowledge creation and work system transfer.

Cross-Cultural Diffusion as Negotiated Change

The pattern of successful diffusion is clear. Negotiated change produces
fewer barriers and more opportunity to create knowledge. Interestingly,
"negotiations" is a term that does not lend itself easily to translation into
Japanese in the manner in which we want to use it.[19] This means that we
need to make certain that our definition of this term is well understood.
As noted earlier, we see negotiations as more than the classic collective
bargaining of traditional U.S. labor relations.

We use an expanded definition of negotiation to capture a wide range
of interactions in which the parties are both creating and claiming value.[20]
This includes complex situations with multiple layers of information
sharing, such as a group problem-solving process. In workplaces where
such complex negotiated interaction occurs, change is an ongoing process of information sharing and knowledge creation.

It is crucial to understand that the channels for communication and
the mechanisms for interaction are embedded in more than just the formal organizational structure. We observed this expanded negotiation
process in a team meeting, over coffee in the cafeteria, and at the bargaining table. The process is analogous to early indigenous innovation.
This reflects the degree to which the individuals involved shape the process by the characteristics they bring to it.

One product of the negotiation process is the creation of a knowledge base distinct to the organization.[21] By definition, this knowledge
continually expands in small and frequently unanticipated ways. People
in these organizations create the patterns of change distinct to the firm.
Individuals and groups bring unique knowledge, experience, and values, which affect the knowledge created within the workplace. This diversity can also create an intense challenge to individual value systems
and perceptions of the environment. We observed how Japanese and
American colleagues devised mutual patterns for problem solving, planning, and "predicting successful courses of action" in order to meet the
challenges they faced.[22]

For example, at NUMMI we discovered problem solving that extended beyond the narrow boundary of the production floor. When we
visited the plant, we were told that one goal was to have the best cafeteria—a cafeteria that was much more than just a place to get food. Contrast this with the old paradigm in which cafeterias were not a priority

and were frequently substandard. Workers in these places found it much more enjoyable to go off site to have lunch. Lunch breaks also provided an opportunity for people to do whatever they could to escape the tensions of the workplace. This sometimes meant alcohol or illegal drugs. Under GM management, the plant experienced serious substance abuse problems. The NUMMI response was to create a place that people enjoyed. The food was good, and the environment encouraged socializing among the workers.

Establishing a high-quality cafeteria provided NUMMI with several important benefits. It helped to avoid the substance abuse problems of the earlier period, workers were afforded nutritious food at a reasonable cost, and the cafeteria served as a channel for ongoing communication among all employees. The physical setup of the cafeteria, just as in open offices or hotspots, was also significant. Most of the tables were round and not bolted to the floor. People moved the furniture to sit together during lunchtime, thus providing another opportunity for negotiation of the details that make up a workplace culture.

Negotiated change processes also occur at other levels such as between two firms, a firm and a union, a firm and its workers, or a firm and a community. For example, at Denso Manufacturing–Michigan, Inc., a multitude of negotiations went on as the company set up its factory in Battle Creek. Stan Tooley and James Heddinger documented the events in this process in their book where they talk of a blending of the two systems that has led to a unique management and corporate culture at Nippondenso. They note that it has produced "a unique company—not really American, but certainly not Japanese."[23] At every turn, major decisions as well as minor details were discussed. This may not always be recognized and identified as negotiation. However, as the cultures and people came together they had to make choices and resolve a myriad of important potential misunderstandings.

This ability to make choices and resolve conflicts across cultures is illustrated very well by another story we were told about the development of a negotiated culture at this same Denso Manufacturing–Michigan, Inc., plant. Mr. Michio (Henry) Ohiwa, the first president, insisted the company avoid the notion of an "American way" and a "Japanese way." Instead, he urged that people just think in terms of "our way." He told us that kaizen was brought to the plant by American team leaders who were sent to Japan and decided that kaizen was the best way of managing the workplace. Mr. Ohiwa, who had been a sales manager for years and was sensitive to cultural tension, had not used this term in order to avoid stereotypical Japanese management. The U.S. team leaders urged the company to use the concept of kaizen, and Mr. Ohiwa agreed to their proposal to make it the main conceptual tool at Denso Manu-facturing–Michigan, Inc.

Once the term kaizen was adopted, the diffusion story did not stop there. In 1992 the then president of Denso U.S.A., Mr. Mineo (Sam) Kawai, stated that the most important accomplishment at Denso was what he termed the "standardization" of the procedures associated with kaizen. He said that these principles, which were strongly advocated by his predecessor, Mr. Ohta, "have firmly taken root here." This was important, not only as an accomplishment in its own right, but also because of the ways that it enabled other progress. Specifically, he em-phasized that the idea has expanded beyond production to include qual-ity, safety, and "quality of work life" as important areas for continuous improvement.

The process of determining what is and is not negotiable is com-plex and not always self-evident. Mr. Kaiwa stated, for example, that "we must keep committed to our philosophy of mutual understanding, mu-tual trust and mutual respect. Denso hats are a symbol. Although some people suggest we remove the obligation to wear hats, I will not budge in this regard. My saying is that as president of this company I am per-sonally committed to this policy and when I see our people wear the hats, I feel more responsible for the well-being of them." On its surface, this position on part of a company uniform seems surprisingly firm. Yet it is clear that an employee's willingness to wear the hat is taken as a visible sign of commitment that is met in a reciprocal way by management.

In this respect, the entire diffusion process requires countless jour-neys beneath the superficial meaning of choices and preferences. In this case, Mr. Kaiwa went on to state that "of course, we have to be flexible enough to blend our philosophy and technology with practices and value systems here." He stated that "I always tell my Japanese people here that, as a foreigner, we are allowed to be here only based on the goodwill of people in this country and we have to be part of the community. I am proud of the fact that more than 400 of our people, including most of the Japanese families, participated in the 'Walk for America' last year despite rain."

In a first-wave site such as Hitachi Magnetics, the changes were deliberately not focused on the introduction of major innovation, but there were still many points at which beliefs and values clashed and needed to be reconciled. Japanese managers may not have attempted to intro-duce entire work organization systems, but they still faced the fact that there were few mechanisms to facilitate the acceptance of new practices. It is true that cross-cultural interaction was enabled at Hitachi in the form of a regular softball game where management competed against the workers, but the work to be done in untangling these issues goes well beyond what can be explored in this sort of setting.

In a situation where change is necessary for business survival, a common language or set of behaviors must be developed. For example, during the early startup at AAI a worker was injured and Japanese executives immediately visited the workstation to see what caused the injury. The American foremen were angry because they felt that the impromptu visit by upper management seemed to cast doubt on their ability to handle the situation and challenged their authority. It was necessary to explain to the Americans that it was a common practice for Japanese executives to investigate a shop-floor injury. Information sharing is one part of an expanded definition of negotiation. These interactions provide a mechanism to resolve the differences in cultural expectations. What must be apparent here is the value of these negotiated and intangible elements to the success of the business.

Shared Knowledge and Context

Cross-cultural diffusion inevitably challenges people to learn about each other. As people interact, assumptions surface. In the process of learning about others, each also contemplates his or her own image in a mirror.[24] Through these interactions and the knowledge that is created, the gap in shared assumptions can be ignored, narrowed, or widened.

For example, when a U.S. and a Japanese manager meet, they have several options for greeting each other. They can either shake hands or bow. The choice they make may well depend on the context in which they meet. If they meet in Japan, they are more likely to bow. If they meet in the United States, they are more likely to shake hands. In the context of a Japanese-affiliated factory located in the United States, the choice is not so clear. It is even possible that they will identify some new form of greeting or a combination of the two. Also, through trial and error (a form of negotiation) they will adjust subtleties such as just how long to shake hands, how firmly to do so, and how low to bow.

In sorting through mutual expectations, individuals begin to construct a set of shared understandings. The tangible part of this type of interaction, which is the actual greeting, is only one dimension of the negotiation process. A much more complex dimension of the interaction concerns the intangibles. In this instance, the intangibles include the uncertainty and discomfort caused by changes in our patterned ways of interacting. Reaction to this uncertainty may also reveal the knowledge stored away about cultural greetings and may involve the emergence of new patterns of explicit knowledge around how to interact.

These moments of shared knowledge creation take place in the larger context that we have discussed in the earlier parts of this chapter. There is an overall structure, which includes being in a primary, secondary, or reverse diffusion situation. Then there are different strategies for diffusion, including negotiated and imposed approaches. As important as these strategies and structures are, they alone will not account for the successful or unsuccessful diffusion of work practices.

When we visited many of the second-wave U.S. locations, we were struck by the degree to which the shop floor was neat, clean, and orderly. In contrast, in many U.S. factories in the steel or auto supply industries it is common to see oil, metal scrap, and package wrappings on the floor and inventory scattered about. We noticed that the way things were organized on the shop floor at Denso Manufacturing–Michigan, Inc., in Battle Creek had the same feel as the way things were organized in the Denso Nishio plant. Likewise, at the Nagoya Steel Works of Nippon Steel the organization of inventory and materials was similar to what we observed at I/NTek.

These clean and orderly work areas reflect the underlying influence of the five S's. Although the five S's are Japanese concepts, American workers have begun to incorporate them into their daily work routines. Contrast work practices at the GM Fremont plant with those used today by the same workers at NUMMI. Activities such as always putting the right tool in the right place, cleaning oil off machines, or doing the same motion in the same way were not characteristic of operations at the GM Fremont plant. What sounds like a simple set of behaviors is really a complex change process that influenced many decisions made by Japanese engineers and managers as they worked to lay out the shop floor and arrange inventory. But something more was required before these new behaviors became part of the way work was done on a daily basis.

At first, the behaviors were learned and repeated as routine parts of the tasks. People almost certainly did not think of themselves as performing tangible tasks that were expressions of intangible concepts. Yet they did understand that something more was at stake than just doing their job in a new way. A worker commented, for example, that the process of putting things in the right place at work was changing the way she organized things at home—that it was a different way of thinking and a different way of doing things. These intangible elements take on the greatest importance in the knowledge-driven work system.

Like the five S's, other concepts such as kaizen have been introduced in these locations. Each of these concepts is important to the operation of the production system. Each is made of tangible and intangible components. It is not enough merely to teach workers new behaviors; the crucial element is the actual internalization of the meanings of these behaviors. This is a true process of knowledge creation. Therefore, none of these practices would be readily apparent to anyone just benchmarking the tangibles. But the process of cross-cultural diffusion is important in ways that go far beyond these specific concepts or practices.

In an organization in which it is important to diffuse knowledge on a regular basis, it is necessary to build capability around the diffusion process itself. One way to build this capability is to develop mechanisms that promote knowledge creation. For example, a kaizen-teian suggestion program encourages interactions among many parties. Such interactions may occur in a team or across functional areas and corporate levels. Each time information is exchanged, potentially important knowledge is created. In the case of kaizen, this knowledge is used to facilitate incremental change. Over the long term, this incremental change produces cumulative change that may have a major impact. The potential for change is apparent when we compare the details of a production process at Denso Manufacturing–Michigan, Inc., in Battle Creek with the line at the Nishio plant. Twenty years of small incremental changes have resulted in standardized work that produces high-quality products at lower cost while maximizing the ways that individual workers add value.

The process of creating shared knowledge is a process of challenging assumptions. In this process, a depth of prior experience is invaluable—so long as it isn't rigidly held. For example, Toyota had many decades of experience with its work system, and the former GM workers at NUMMI had many decades of experience with a very different work system. The diffusion process in this case was enabled by Toyota's confidence in its work system, the unfreezing effect of the plant shutdown, and the skillful introduction of a new way of doing things. The workers had a shared frame of reference around how they know work should not be, which facilitated dialogue and adoption of a new system that was more effective. By contrast, Denso Manufacturing–Michigan, Inc., had a new workforce with relatively little shared experience in manufacturing. They did have confidence in their work system. As Mr. Mineo (Sam) Kawai, the third president of this operation, commented, when they came to the United States, "We had built enough self-confidence in our way of doing business." He added, "I have been in the heating and cooling business for more than 20 years. When I started my career, such U.S. products as GM-Harrison radiator were just superb and our only hope was to catch up to them as close as possible. After 20 years of enormous effort, we now find we are doing better than our model companies in the early days." Thus, the workforce here had to be educated about the nature of a manufacturing work system. They were not hampered by assumptions about old ways of doing things, but neither were they enabled by a common frame of reference to build on.

Underlying the process in both cases are factors such as mechanisms to create shared knowledge; the acceptance of change as an essential and even welcome part of daily operations; openness to a diversity of perspectives; and recognition that multiple perspectives are all legitimate. A growing degree of trust is built over time through communication, assurances of employment security, and links to a larger social contract. The process that is set in motion involves a succession of interactions in which new forms of homogeneity are created out of diversity. In turn, this homogeneity generates new diversity that becomes the foundation for yet newer forms of homogeneity.

Knowledge: Part of the Intangible Foundation for Global Diffusion

Knowledge has become one of the most powerful forces of competitive advantage in today's marketplace. Creating knowledge effectively for a company or a union is not a simple or well-understood process even for the people in some of the places we visited. They are not unusual. Despite a number of new books on knowledge-creating organizations, the details are few and far between. We have attempted to spell out some potentially helpful ideas and processes as well as a few stumbling blocks.

Knowledge creation is a dynamic force linked with ongoing and relentless change in new production systems. To effectively create and use knowledge, firms must understand the forces that can support or destroy it. In groups where virtual knowledge is created, it must be directed toward a collective goal. This allows the creation of explicit knowledge, which can be used to solve problems, fix a machine, negotiate a contract, or perform any number of work-related tasks. The people in the sites we visited are actively using knowledge they create to alter or adapt their work and work environments. The work organization system, the management philosophy, and the modes of interaction available are all factors in this negotiated and incremental change process.

In a process in which the whole is greater than the sum of the parts, small changes can extend or destroy the intended product. Factors such as a change in process, group composition, information sources or a shift in levels of organizational trust can alter the knowledge-creation process. The individual contributions of the people in a group all have an impact on the collective product. If one of those people is absent or if a new person comes into the group, the nature of the virtual knowledge, as well as the subsequent explicit knowledge derived from it, is changed.

Everett Rogers asserts that diffusion is the outcome of a pattern-making process in which shared understandings and mutual agreements exist.[25] Individuals are linked by "patterned flows" of information. Rogers says that in this way information processing creates structures. The nature of the structure coupled with factors such as homogeneity or physical space may well determine the success of the organization through both formal and informal networks. We believe that kaizen, meetings, and teams are far more than just elements of work organization; they are among the shop-floor-level mechanisms that create the structure necessary for the diffusion of innovation, information, and knowledge.

It is perhaps difficult to understand how a knowledge-driven production system that creates solid metal machinery can so depend on elements that we describe as intangible and fragile. Obviously, the physical components of the production line are tangible and sturdy. They support the weight of materials and labor. Once again we must look at the intangible nature of a process in order to understand its fragility. Interdependencies among the system components are crucial. For example, JIT delivery from suppliers must be successful, or production stops for lack of parts. There are few physical buffers such as in-process inventory that can be used to maintain production. People provide the most substantial buffers and facilitate the ongoing leanness of such a system. These people are regular as well as temporary workers used to adjust labor costs while providing an essential source of knowledge and experience. Workers absorb shocks to the system and allow it to be responsive through constant awareness and adjustment. Diffusion of information and knowledge creation are vital elements of this effort.

4

Team-Based Work Systems

· ·

Companies in every industry are striving to create team-based work systems.[1] Few are achieving the new levels of teamwork they believe will make them more competitive. For many of these firms, the interest in teams has roots in the competitive success of many Japanese organizations, which feature high levels of teamwork in manufacturing and office operations. Team-based work systems are complex amalgams of tangible practices and intangible elements such as interpersonal interactions. Achieving the proper mix of these components pays large dividends in increased organizational effectiveness, which we believe depends in part on the creation of knowledge within the firm. By taking a closer look at the ways the organizations we visited have introduced team-based work systems, we can learn valuable lessons.

In our research, we found that it was inaccurate to place all work organization systems in these Japanese-affiliated manufacturing operations into a single category. While all eight organizations that we studied reported having teams, we found three very different types of team-based work systems. In this chapter, we will summarize earlier findings and extend them to focus on some of the intangible but essential factors that influence the cross-cultural diffusion of a team-based work system.[2] We will also highlight the importance of negotiated change in the diffusion process as well as in regular functioning of team-based work systems.

Our analysis of these three types of teams centers initially on the two waves of Japanese investment, forms of ownership (joint venture versus wholly owned subsidiary), and the type of work system in place. These factors are helpful in explaining the diversity of teams we found. However, we will reach beyond these explanations to consider intangibles that are essential in the successful implementation of a team-based work system. This is especially true with the added complexity of transferring this knowledge from work areas in one country to work areas in another.

Explaining the Variation in Team Systems

Given the observed range of team-based work systems in the Japanese-owned and U.S.–Japanese joint-venture plants, how do we account for the variation? While no single factor can explain all of what we observed, four factors are helpful in understanding the story. Three of these are structural factors: the timing of the Japanese investment in the United States, the ownership structure, and the technological constraints on the work system. In chapter 3, we classified the eight factories according to each of the three factors (table 3.1). In this chapter, we examine each of these factors to account for the diversity of types of teams in these organizations. But these structural factors alone do not fully explain the dynamics involved in the cross-cultural diffusion at these facilities. A fourth critical factor, the intangibles, became apparent after we recognized that the tangible, structural ones were inadequate. Intangible elements include discipline, trust, knowledge, stress, fear, and patterns of interaction. They are always present, may be constructive, and shape the tangible elements they accompany. For example, fear of losing a job may stop a worker from proposing suggestions that streamline the work process. Tangible and intangible elements form a dynamic tension, which is often unidentified and not well understood.

Production systems are forced to focus on objective or tangible measures. Accordingly, organizational reward systems depend largely on measurable outcomes. Although people are a vital part of any production system, especially team-based systems, managers frequently focus on measurable items rather than on the intangibles, which promote the effective performance of workers.

The interdependency between tangible and intangible elements must be recognized, and we offer some insights into this relationship in the following section. For example, within STS teams intangibles such as team autonomy allow a high level of interaction within the team and independence from the upstream and downstream production operations. In lean production, teams are interdependent because of the linkages of shared information and knowledge as well as the physical interconnectedness of work. To explain these details, we will describe the basic elements of our ideas.

Three Types of Team-Based Work Systems

When we began our field research, we did not make fine distinctions about types of work organizations and forms of worker participation. Every one of the sites characterized itself as featuring team-based work systems, and we did not have in mind any specific distinctions among types of teams. We had read the MIT auto study report entitled *The Machine That Changed the World*, which coined the term "lean production" to identify a fundamental shift from the dominant paradigm of mass production. We expected to find examples of the lean production system among all the Japanese production facilities, and we anticipated that union status would be a key factor in examining work organization and participation issues.

After a series of site visits and hundreds of interviews,[3] we observed far more variation in the forms of work organizations than was accounted for by anything we had read in the literature. While the unionized sites certainly faced distinct challenges and opportunities as a result of their union status, the different types of work systems bridged both union and nonunion settings.

In this section, we will focus on the tangible elements of team-based systems. We have classified the plants in this study into three types of work systems, traditional, STS, and lean, each of which features three distinct forms of work teams.

We visited four plants that we immediately recognized as being lean production facilities. Lean teams are a core component of this production system. They are tightly linked to the way work is performed through elements such as in-process inventory control, internal customers, and on-line quality control. An important aspect of this on-line control is the ability to stop the production process without fear of reprisal. These teams had dedicated meeting places in which they maintained tracking charts, defect reports, safety data, and attendance records, which are all part of the visual factory.[4] An additional tangible element of lean teams is a dedicated team leader whose responsibility is expanded to include the entire production process. The teams are relatively small, with an average size of five to seven people.

Two of our plants looked more like STS initiatives than lean production operations. They featured an autonomous team structure much like those pioneered in England and Sweden. Sociotechnical systems teams typically absorb supervisory duties such as scheduling of training and vacations and budgeting. One of the most tangible elements of STS systems is the existence of a variety of buffers throughout the process—

which contrasts with lean teams. Buffers can include continuous production technology, a pool of temporary employees, and extra in-process inventory.

Finally, the two first-wave sites are traditional U.S. manufacturing plants that are at various stages of restructuring their work systems. These plants feature off-line teams, including quality circles, employee involvement groups, task forces, and labor–management committees. These types of teams are not directly connected to the production process. Members take on teamwork in addition to their regular organizational duties. The tangible elements include an ad hoc membership structure with team meetings off line and separate from their "normal work" activities.

Two Forms of Ownership

The four firms featuring lean manufacturing work systems were established in the 1980s, and they reflect a much higher level of diffusion of Japanese work practices. The first two entries in the second wave, NUMMI and AAI (Mazda), were joint ventures. They provide us with illustrations of corporate-level decisions aimed specifically at knowledge creation and learning.

Particularly in the case of NUMMI, the ownership structure reflected a desire on the part of both partners to learn from one another. General Motors sought to learn more about the Toyota production system. At the same time, Toyota sought to learn about the U.S. unionized workforce, the legal system, and other local issues relevant to expanding manufacturing capacity in North America. In both cases, extensive planning preceded the actual ramp up of production. Representatives from all the parties met to establish parameters for activities that would meet each party's interests. Interactions of this nature fit into our description of negotiation.

Although it may not have been acknowledged, learning was occurring in this procedure. We believe that this learning enables much smoother progress toward the establishment of successful business operations. As a result, these joint ventures represent a much higher degree of diffusion of Japanese work practices as well as increased confidence of Japanese managers in their work system and the willingness of U.S. workers to adopt it.

The establishment of NUMMI focused on the transfer of the work system employed at Toyota's Takaoka plant in Japan, while Mazda brought the systems from their Hiroshima plant. These are early examples of Japanese firms that intended to transplant or impose their work systems. Both were affiliated with local partners, GM and Ford, who wanted to facilitate the creation of new jobs and effective business procedures. In addition, the experiences at NUMMI helped to dispel concerns about the capacity of the U.S. workforce to adopt a new production system.

The wholly owned subsidiaries in the second wave of Japanese investment followed at later dates. It is likely that U.S. trade policy and other competitive pressures made being closer to the U.S. market very attractive.

Denso Manufacturing–Michigan, Inc., for example, is part of the Toyota *keiretsu* system.[5] Both Toyota and Denso Japan have opened multiple facilities in the United States. It is possible that these companies learned from their own as well as each other's experiences. For example, the NUMMI experience had a direct influence on Toyota's plan to transplant its work system to Georgetown, Kentucky, and on Denso Japan's initial decision to locate in Battle Creek.

Within what we have termed the second wave of investment are two additional firms that do not utilize lean manufacturing principles. The Coil Center and I/NTek were classified as STS facilities. A close look at these joint ventures reveals that it was the U.S. side of each partnership that emphasized the STS-style autonomy. At the Coil Center, the team structure that emphasized extended job rotation and cross training was introduced primarily by the American who was the initial general manager of the business. At I/NTek, the steelworkers union agreed to be part of a joint governance structure and played a key role in emphasizing team autonomy.

Thus, the two STS facilities were joint ventures where the U.S. partners were the driving forces in establishing the employment relations systems. This provides some evidence to suggest that an STS approach, which is not typically found in Japan, will be more likely to be utilized in the context of a U.S.-dominated joint venture. However, if joint venture status helps to account for the existence of the STS sites, it does not guarantee that an STS approach will be utilized: two other joint ventures utilized lean production systems. To explain the mix of STS and lean production teams, we must examine the primary production process in these locations.

Production Technology Constraints

The original conception of sociotechnical systems optimized two overlapping subsystems, the social and the technical. In practice, STS interventions emphasize one primary social system, which centers on autonomous work teams to address the assumed core human needs for influence and autonomy. A key requirement for autonomous work teams is some form of buffer between teams. Buffers could include inventory, highly discrete tasks, or operation on separate shifts. Observers have pointed out that the utilization of lean production and total quality management principles such as JIT delivery and reduced inventory between operations removes buffers that are critical to team autonomy.[6] Thus, when we found two U.S.–Japanese joint ventures operating with STS teams, we took a close look at the production system constraints.

In our analysis of production systems, we will be distinguishing among the three broad modes of production—assembly, batch, and continuous.[7] Examining the classification of our cases by production system reveals that three assembly operations are utilizing lean production teams and that one features off-line teams. The traditional notion of off-line teams has roots in the U.S. auto industry, where quality of worklife (QWL) and employee involvement teams were pioneered in the 1970s and have been used extensively since then. Lean production has been identified as a flexible and effective way to produce goods.[8] It is no surprise that we found both traditional off-line and newer lean production teams in the four assembly operations. In contrast, we would expect tensions to arise where STS-type teams were established in manufacturing settings operating on a lean production basis.

Only one of our cases, I/NTek, involves a continuous manufacturing process. Historically, continuous production settings have been the sites of the best documented STS cases.[9] This may reflect the relatively small number of staff associated with a particular production operation or required on a given shift. As a result, all of the workers on a shift or in a work operation can be established as an autonomous team. Thus, it was not surprising to find an STS team in such a setting. The principles of lean production (such as JIT delivery, standardized work operations, and reduced in-process inventory) would not be as applicable.

The balance of the cases has been classified as batch production, and here we find all three types of team systems. The fact that one of the firms had traditional off-line teams is not a surprise since these types of team structures are broadly diffused across a wide range of work settings in North America. We already know that the concept can be utilized in batch production as well as in assembly operations. However, the existence of different types of teams at Ogihara (lean) and Coil Center (STS) is most interesting. This is especially true because both are metal stamping operations employing very similar technologies and are located within a few miles of one another. As we saw in the earlier discussion of ownership structures, the STS system at Coil Center reflected the influence of the U.S. manager. The work system choice at Ogihara is more complex to trace, since the firm owns die-making rather than stamping operations in Japan.

The production technology helps to explain the tendencies toward one or another type of team system. Assembly operations lend themselves to lean and off-line teams, while continuous production lends itself to STS teams.[10] Batch production technologies can be organized around all three types of team systems, revealing a high degree of flexibility in social structures. Our findings confirm the original notion of sociotechnical systems even as they point to the limits on the autonomous structures that have become accepted STS practice. In the following section, we will compare three types of team systems across a number of factors.

Comparison of Three Types of Team Systems

We have described different types of teams in relation to the ownership arrangements, the production technology, and the constraints imposed by the investment time periods. These broad characteristics are not enough to explain the dynamics at the shop-floor or team level. It is important to examine the details of each type of team.

If we examine the details listed in table 4.1, we can identify several major trends. For example, off-line teams are described as separate from the production process (an adjunct to the structure of the organization) and come into being to solve problems on an ad hoc basis. In other words, they are not integral to the production process, which limits their ability to create and share knowledge with the entire organization. This separateness does not facilitate interaction between these teams and other segments of the firm.

Sociotechnical systems teams, by comparison, are linked to production and have high levels of team member interdependence. Since STS teams complete an entire process, they are not linked strongly to upstream suppliers or downstream customers. In addition, they have high levels of team autonomy. Unlike members of off-line teams, the members of STS teams share a common work area. These characteristics encourage information sharing and knowledge creation within the team. The self-managing nature of an STS team also can encourage high levels of interaction among the team members. The high levels of interaction can have positive and negative consequences. Some teams' performance will suffer due to peer pressure and group think, while other teams' performance can be greater than the sum of the parts. The strong links within the team may make it resistant to new ideas and to attempts to negotiate change from the outside.

Lean teams are formed in a system in which production buffers are minimized so that the team is tightly linked to internal customers and

Table 4.1   A Comparison of Three Types of Team Systems

	Lean production teams	Sociotechnical systems teams	Off-line teams
Origins	Japan (Toyota Pull System, 1960s)	Scandinavia (Volvo, Kalmar, Sweden, 1970s) and England (coal mines, 1940s)	United States (Harmon and GM/UAW quality of worklife groups, 1970s) and Japan (quality circles, 1980s)
System optimizes	Continuous improvement in work operations	Mix of social and technical subsystems	Ad hoc problem solving
Expected yield	Systematic gains in quality, productivity, and cost	Increased worker commitment and targeted gains in quality and safety	Increased worker commitment and reactive response to quality problems
Success constrained by	High expectations of team autonomy; low labor/management support for continuous improvement	High levels of team interdependence; limited resources for technical redesign	Separation from daily operations
Typically found in	Assembly operations (high interdependency among teams)	Continuous production operations (high autonomy among teams)	Broad range of workplaces
Leadership	Depends on strong team leader	Depends on self-managing group	Depends on group facilitator
Membership	Common work area	Common work area	May draw on multiple work areas
Organization structure	Core building block	Core building block	Adjunct to the structure
Links to other teams	Tightly linked to internal customers and suppliers within each shift as well as across shifts	Tightly linked across shifts; loosely linked with other teams	Little or no links among teams

suppliers.[11] Autonomy is constrained because lean teams require strong leadership at the shop-floor level. Supervisors and team leaders are vital communication links between teams and the rest of the organization. In this setting, the teams are interdependent and must negotiate potential changes or improvements. Incremental systemwide change depends on robust and yet sensitive information sharing. The flow of information must be continuous since any change has an immediate impact on other parts of the organization. Therefore, lean teams are effective because their focus on business goals facilitates knowledge creation and learning across the firm.

In STS and lean production firms, the type of team structure is a core component of the organizational system. Furthermore, the type of team that exists will have a great impact on the level of organizational knowledge creation and negotiated change. It is crucial to keep in mind the interaction of the team with other elements of the production system as well as larger organizational constraints.

Intangibles

It is common practice for corporations to copy only the tangible parts of successful production systems they have seen at other places. These attempts typically produce disappointing results. They fail to recognize that the intangible elements are integral to the operation of the system. For example, esprit de corps among teams is difficult to both develop and replicate. Members of a team can develop interdependency, trust, and shared knowledge, but their experience is unique to a specific workplace, context, and group of people.

Firms in the United States have traditionally valued and protected technology, capital, buildings, and machinery. In mass production, the machines are designed in ways that determine people's participation in production. In knowledge-driven production, people determine the machines' participation in production. Mass production is designed to minimize disruption by intangibles, while lean production thrives on maximizing the value of the intangibles that people bring to the system.

The consequences of the inability of companies to transfer these unique intangibles can be best illustrated by two auto assembly plants with lean production systems, AAI (Mazda) and NUMMI. They have nearly identical tangible components, such as similar team meeting areas, doors-off assembly, low in-process inventory, kaizen-teian programs, and andon systems. In addition, both firms have contracts with the UAW that govern compensation and benefits. However, there were palpable differences in the processes and outcomes of each site.

We observed a major difference in the degree to which the employees were engaged in the system. At AAI (Mazda), meeting areas were used primarily for social conversations during breaks. Team members at NUMMI used similar areas as information centers with updated charts on quality, cost, training, safety, and other aspects of the business. These up-to-date charts provide tangible data to support team feedback, evaluation, and strategic planning. This allows the teams to focus their efforts by combining current data with their knowledge of company goals.

In the introduction of an STS system, companies also need to highlight more of the intangible elements than would be the case in a traditional system. For example, two sites were classified as STS facilities: Coil Center and I/NTek. Compared to the system at Coil Center, the system at I/NTek was designed to enable employees to have much more voice in the entire process. From the beginning I/NTek workers were full participants in the details of designing the work organization. Therefore, they have a greater sense of ownership, pride, and participation—all key intangibles.

At Coil Center, the work structure was primarily based on the ideas and input of the original American manager. Although the initial group of employees received over 100 days of training, they apparently had little input in the design of the system. The leadership approach proved inconsistent to sustain the intended team design.

Emphasis on intangible elements builds a climate that is oriented toward process rather than toward outcome. Focus on process can be healthy for the organization and the people involved because it encourages flexibility, builds adaptability, and creates a mechanism for change. Therefore, intangible factors such as knowledge creation, information sharing, and interdependency can create a self-reinforcing cycle.

Such a self-reinforcing cycle can be seen in the kaizen process. Small incremental improvements start the process of knowledge creation. If workers make suggestions and see them implemented promptly, they learn that their ideas are taken seriously. In a team-based system, this can begin a rippling effect. As workers see changes occur, they may be able to propose more ideas that continue to improve the original idea. Teams begin to see how their suggestions and actions affect the work organization system.

This interplay, which expands the role of the intangibles, is illustrated in figure 4.1. The interaction between tangible and intangible elements of a work system takes place on many levels and in many ways. Consider the process by which worker suggestions are generated and implemented. Figure 4.1 is highly simplified and focused on just some parts of one activity—suggestion making. The process components in the center of the figure represent tangibles. These include a worker or a team making a suggestion, the generation of a work order and other activities associated with implementing the suggestion, and the resulting improvements in daily operations. Improvements can include cost cuts, waste reductions, improved safety, skill acquisition, and achievement of goals.

There are also intangible parts of this process, which are depicted in the figure with cloud-like boundaries. These include the way that a worker or a team suggestion adds to a shared knowledge base and the way an implemented suggestion furthers learning of the worker or team and oth-

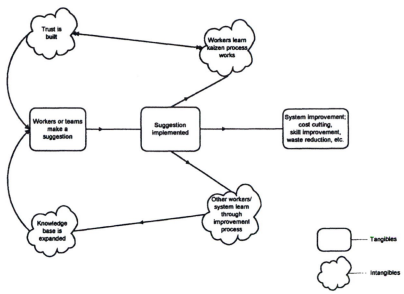

Figure 4.1 A simplified illustration of the interaction between tangibles and intangibles.

ers. Intangibles are also the main ingredients for building trust and social contracts among the various stakeholders. Similar interactions can be identified around tangible and intangible aspects of quality, maintenance, customer service, financial accounting, training, dispute resolution, materials management, and countless other aspects of daily operations.

Conclusion

For nearly a century, American workplaces have been dominated by the logic of Taylorism, according to which individual variability was to be engineered out of jobs to achieve standardization deemed essential to serve growing mass markets. At the same time, organizations were dominated by a comparable bureaucratic logic, by which tasks and responsibilities were progressively subdivided to minimize risk and responsibility. As we look to the next century, production systems and organizations are turning this logic on its head. We see the emergence of work systems premised on harnessing the knowledge that is closest to the source, at the point where products are made or services are delivered. In these new knowledge-driven workplaces, teams are the essential platform on which individual ideas surface and are constructively woven into daily operations.

In summary, we wish to emphasize the following points. First, the team structure has to match the technical constraints of the production system. For example, a system with reduced inventory buffers will constrain STS or traditional forms of team autonomy. More specifically, the tangible elements of a lean production system limit an intangible one such as autonomy under STS.

Second, the flow of information is an intangible element that operates very differently under each team system. In the traditional model, there is limited information flow, and most of it occurs outside the team. Under STS, there is increased information flow but within the team. With lean production, there is extensive information flow within the team as well as between the team and the larger system. This further illustrates the way in which intangibles are interdependent with production systems.

Third, while off-line teams at our traditional locations are diffused in a piecemeal fashion, STS and lean team systems require a more comprehensive approach. In both, the tangible and intangible elements of the team-based system are interdependent. As a result, the piecemeal diffusion of tangible elements will always produce disappointing results.

Effective team-based work depends upon the unseen tension between the tangible and intangible elements. At organizational levels, these same forces are at work. Without employment security and human resource policies that facilitate the knowledge-creation process, teams cannot realize their full potential. The energy this tension produces can propel systems forward or destroy their effectiveness.

5

Employee Involvement
and Kaizen

. . . .

Success in the global economy depends on understanding how
people's knowledge is integrated into work operations. Despite plati-
tudes about how "people are our most important resource," most organizations do not attend to these details. As a result, they fail to realize the
full benefit of the knowledge of their employees. This failure arises out of
the ineffective handling of a series of interrelated workplace dilemmas.

First, there is a fundamental dilemma that arises around a manager's
desire for involvement or input, on the one hand, and a manager's need
for control and accountability, on the other. When faced with test events,
most managers opt for control. The continued disregard of employee
knowledge becomes a self-fulfilling prophecy—employees learn not to
make suggestions or share their ideas.

Second, most managers focus on solving discrete problems rather
than on seeking to optimize a work system. But a focus on discrete problems prevents one from seeing the ways in which problems are part of
an interconnected whole. This dilemma is reinforced by a top-down
mindset that finds legitimacy in having "expert" specific problem solving
rather than having employees share information to address root causes.

Third, most managers operate in organizations that place a premium
on short-term results. There is an assumption that increased focus on short-
term results will bring an organization successively closer to its long-term
objectives. Yet just the reverse is true. The long-term vision becomes increasingly remote as a result of a preoccupation with the short term.

The logic of employee involvement centers on the notion that a small
number of managers or other experts do not have enough knowledge to

71

drive the required improvements in operations. The assumption is that as much input from as many people as possible is desirable. Yet this gives rise to a fourth dilemma, which is that more and more input is harder and harder to process. Consider the notion that operations must be standardized if they are to be improved—a concept central to the quality movement. Simply put, with more input it is more difficult to standardize. Yet with less input it is likely that standardization will take place around ideas that are not as well connected to daily workplace realities.

These four dilemmas are ubiquitous. Managers and workers in the organizations we studied faced these dilemmas just as much as people in other organizations. What is interesting is the way in which an appreciation for employee involvement—in the full sense of the term—leads to a very different set of responses to the dilemmas. As Hamel and Prahalad say, "Some firms are just more efficient at learning than others."[1]

The dilemmas are not effectively addressed by the narrow forms of employee involvement found in many organizations, which are focused on traditional suggestions and off-line teams. Similarly, if kaizen or other continuous improvement efforts are seen as little more than "suggestion programs," then they will not address the dilemmas either. It is only when employee knowledge—tacit and explicit—is valued in a work system that the dilemmas are addressed in a meaningful way.

Historical Context

To explain how the dilemmas were addressed in the organizations we studied, we must place them in historical context. Though only a few of the organizations had initiatives that used the "employee involvement" label, the history of the underlying participative principles is applicable to all. Similarly, only a few of the organizations had initiatives that used the term "kaizen," yet the history of the underlying quality principles is universal. In both cases, the history takes on new meaning if we examine it through the twin lenses of a knowledge-driven work system and global diffusion.[2]

The practice of employee involvement took on special meaning after the rise of scientific management and the bureaucratic organization. In the 1940s and 1950s, authors such as McGregor, Homans, Mayo, and Roethlisberger began to call into question an implicit set of assumptions that managers needed to monitor and control employees.[3] They called instead for a more "humanistic" approach that involved soliciting employee views and assuming that most people wanted to do a good job.

In the early 1970s, U.S. employers looked beyond individual motivation programs[4] and sought to harness the ideas and energies of employee groups. It was in this context that we saw the rise of "quality of worklife," sociotechnical systems, and the total quality management movement. The proponents of these principles were rallying against what they saw as oppressive and limiting management approaches.

The principles of employee involvement took shape in the 1970s under the banner of "quality of worklife" (QWL) as off-line teams began to be established in many industries. Barry and Irving Bluestone described early attempts to negotiate for QWL in the late 1960s at General Motors.[5] Ford followed later with the term "employee involvement," and most firms in the steel industry used the term "labor-management participation teams."

From a diffusion perspective, QWL and the other forms of off-line involvement extended to a substantial number of workplaces. Some studies at the time estimated that more than half of all medium-sized and large organizations in the United States had some form of participative program. This rapid diffusion reflected the facts that relatively little change was required in daily operations and that some noticeable improvements occurred in the early stages of the initiatives.

As employees began to build capability to make improvements in the workplace, however, the organizations were not ready to reinforce and build on this capability. As a result, employee ideas about how to redesign work ran up against the assumption that knowledge and expertise on these core issues still had to come down from the top. Once employees learned that the message was involvement, but only on incidental issues, the momentum of many initiatives was lost. The high failure rate among such initiatives is not surprising. These early QWL groups had an advantage over the individual-based incentive programs by virtue of channeling group energies, but they were still "add-on" programs.

In the case of sociotechnical systems, the early scholars, such as Eric Trist, called for an approach to what was then mass production technology that took into account the social needs and capabilities of the workforce.[6] The result, as we saw in our discussion of teams, was a series of important pilot experiments beginning in Britain's postwar coal fields and extending in the 1960s and 1970s to organizations such as Volvo (Kalmar, Sweden), Gainsburger Pet Foods (Topeka, Kansas), and the Sarnia chemical plant of Shell Canada Products Ltd. (Sarnia, Ontario). In these and other organizations, autonomous work groups demonstrated their ability to shoulder the responsibility for most aspects of daily workplace operations.

From a diffusion perspective, the STS history is interesting in that the principles emerged through a series of remarkably similar pilot experiments in England, Sweden, the United States, and Canada. Equally interesting is that the pilot experiments may have diffused well across cultures but did not diffuse well within the organizations where they were set up. A closer look at the role of knowledge in these settings reveals that the autonomous nature of the teams concentrated most of the ideas about improvement within the team. As a result, there was not as much capability built around integrating lessons learned in one work area with lessons learned in others—a knowledge base that is essential for diffusion from the part to the whole.

Beginning in the 1950s in Japan, there was the parallel rise of what came to be known as the Toyota production system and total quality control. While these systems involved high levels of employee involvement, they were not driven by the logic of participation or even by the principle of optimizing the social and the technical. Instead, the underlying principles centered on the elimination of waste. Toyota focused on cutting waste and standardizing their operations through suggestions by frontline employees.

Taiichi Ohno's analysis of the Toyota production system highlights the ways in which people's input is central to the operation of this system.[7] Our own research also points to people—more than the technical or mechanical components—as the cornerstone of effective production systems. It is important to understand that the employee involvement highlighted by Ohno, which has been linked to the term "kaizen," is very different from the off-line employee involvement or QWL groups that became so common in the United States in the 1980s.

We use "kaizen" with caution. Among Japanese scholars, the term has been defined in a wide range of ways. For example, Imai defines kaizen quite broadly to include "continuing improvement in personal life, home life, social life, and working life. When applied to the workplace, kaizen means continuing improvement involving everyone—managers and workers alike. The kaizen philosophy assumes that our way of life—be it our working life, our social life or our home life *deserves* to be constantly improved."[8] At the other extreme, Ohno emphasizes just the reduction of non-value-added waste in between the time an order is placed for a product and the time cash is received.[9] Monden has a similar focus on cost reduction.[10]

Of course, the *kanji* characters or ideographs for kaizen in Japanese and Chinese lend themselves to many definitions. Kaizen is composed of a kanji character for "kai," which has connotations of change for the better, and "zen," which has connotations of positive improvement. It has only been applied in the workplace context within the past 50 years, which is where the notions of incremental change have been added.

In using the term, we are mindful that kaizen has come to be associated with Toyota. At a site such as Denso Manufacturing–Michigan, Inc., this is a favorable association due to close links with Toyota. On the other hand, at a site such as Ogihara they emphasize that their focus is not on kaizen per se but on total preventive maintenance. Ogihara does place great value on employee involvement, employee suggestions, and a structured process of incremental improvement but does not use the word "kaizen" to describe these elements. Then there are American firms, such as United Technologies, that have adopted the word as central to their corporate strategy but are using it with a meaning much closer to what is termed re-engineering. As was the case with the term "teams," there is no single definition or usage that is common across organizations.

The concept of kaizen is most visible in the form of highly routinized programs to reduce waste and make small incremental improvements. Workers are trained to make proposals that would cut fractions of a second from a movement or save "pennies" in scrap. The full implementation of a kaizen suggestion program takes many years of careful encouragement and training. Everyone in the organization is involved in this effort, and it involves attention all the time, not just once a week in a group meeting.

As we noted earlier in this book, the many integrated principles associated with this work system first diffused to the United States in a piecemeal fashion—as statistical process control, quality circles, JIT delivery, and simultaneous engineering. By the mid 1980s, a more integrated form of these ideas started to diffuse in what came to be known as the quality movement, using terms such as "total quality management," "continuous quality improvement," and the like.

While the quality principles diffused rapidly, the mechanism was typically a directive handed down from management or a customer-driven audit procedure (such as what has now become the ISO 9000 standards). In these contexts, the quality initiatives' more tangible aspects—those having to do with standardization—were reinforced, but the more intangible role of frontline employee knowledge was often lost. The rise of lean production as a concept primarily served to reinforce the focus on tangible work practices.

Thus, even though the QWL, STS, and QC initiatives are all typically lumped together as examples of participative management, we see they are quite distinct when examined through the lenses of diffusion and knowledge-driven work systems. In particular, the role of employee involvement emerges as pivotal, but it is typically mismanaged. The QWL initiatives were right to emphasize participation but never became knowledge driven because they were unprepared for the capability that emerged as employees were trained in problem-solving skills. The STS initiatives were knowledge driven but focused primarily within the team and had difficulty building capability for integration across parts of the system. The quality movement is system oriented but centered primarily on tangible elements of the system. As we turn to the organizations that we studied, we will be taking a close look at the various ways in which the intangible aspects of employee involvement have proven to be central to understanding the diffusion of knowledge-driven work systems.

Knowledge Creation without Employee Involvement

Knowledge creation took place in all of the organizations that we studied, but the process by which this unfolded and the outcomes varied quite a bit. For example, when Hitachi Magnetics, which we have characterized as a mass producer, purchased the GE plant in Edmore, Michigan, the goal was to acquire the most up-to-date technology for magnetics production. Lessons learned about this technology were brought back to Japan; they represent one method of knowledge creation.

Since Hitachi did not intend to introduce new work practices to the plant, the operations in Edmore did not involve an appreciation for the knowledge that workers accumulated through their daily work experiences. This was also an era in which the mass production approach generated profits and seemed highly successful.

The primary challenges to management under this mass production model came through unionization by the workers. In this adversarial relationship, the creation of knowledge was valued, but only the knowledge associated with the separate interests of the employer or the union. It was only when they were faced with a changing marketplace that the U.S. and Japanese managers and union leaders at Hitachi Magnetics began dialogue on their common interests. Still, their dialogue was constrained by the long adversarial history.

Improvement efforts at Hitachi Magnetics centered on the piecemeal introduction of programs and plans that were successful elsewhere. Yet systemic improvements cannot be made in a piecemeal fashion. Without an appreciation for the role of employee involvement, the results are inevitably limited. A vivid example happened at early stages of the drive for improvement at Hitachi Magnetics. After failed attempts at QWL initiatives, the company attempted a Scanlon plan, which offered profit-sharing incentives for measurable gains in performance.

When the plan was established, the company and union agreed through hard bargaining that it needed 93% support from the bargaining unit. When only 92% of employees voted to sustain the effort after the first year, the president decided to drop the program. If the company had wanted to create a strategic incentive for improvement, discontinuing the Scanlon plan delivered the wrong message. The lesson here was based in the traditional mass production management mindset: the letter of the agreement was more important than the involvement of a large majority of the workforce.

When the Scanlon plan at Hitachi Magnetics ended, the parties next tried a relationship-by-objective (RBO) effort with the help of the Federal Mediation and Conciliation Service. As a senior Hitachi manager noted, "We failed in our earlier QWL efforts. There was top support, but no follow-up on suggestions."[11] All three of these efforts had the support of top management but failed to see the importance of true employee involvement.

The apparent lack of commitment to implement changes indicates that the effort was not seen as integral to business operations. Furthermore, it served to reinforce rather than alleviate the cynicism and mistrust in this organization.[12] Thus, the lack of employee involvement at Hitachi Magnetics reflects many decades of operating under a mass production mindset.

When we visited Hitachi, efforts were under way to begin both a kaizen and a suggestion program. Harry Suzuki, a human resources manager, was sent from Japan to help the plant remain competitive. He told us:

> Regarding kaizen and suggestion system, this time we are not asking for member approval. This is top down and we are not in a hurry to implement these two programs. To be successful, we need to make all employees aware of our condition. We need more communication, more monthly meetings with all employees, and more cooperation with all employees.

These comments reflect the company's increased appreciation for employee involvement and its recognition that harnessing employee knowledge was crucial for long-term success.

At Yamaha Musical Products, there was little formal emphasis on employee involvement for very different reasons. We observed individual knowledge creation as the workers built instruments. There was no formal involvement, although people did learn as they identified better ways to do their individual jobs or learned new bid jobs. This learning was not integrated into the overall work practices. For example, one operator commented that he was having trouble with setting parts in the jigs before they were welded. The jigs were loose and it was difficult to properly weld the parts together. The operator developed a new way of adjusting the jigs so that the parts fit better, allowing him to make more consistent welds. As far as we know, however, there were no mechanisms or efforts made to encourage such a worker to discuss the idea with others or to explore its possible application to other operations.

The pressures of competition and rapid product evolution were not as strong in the musical instrument business. This allowed Yamaha to place less emphasis on employee involvement. Yamaha products are recognized as the highest quality in the school musical instrument market, and demand generally outstrips production. It is inevitable that the many people building the instruments could generate additional insights into how to improve quality or reduce waste, but this would also involve a substantial investment in building such capabilities. Future pressures may well increase the value of knowledge creation through employee involvement.

In both of these facilities, there are unions, which can be described as knowledge-creating organizations. It is important to understand that this function exists within a context that is adversarial and focused on the separate interests of the unions, their members, and the firms. The expression of collective voice in a unionized mass production setting is a function of grievances, complaints, and bargaining-table demands. While this is a tightly bounded interaction, knowledge is nonetheless created and acted upon.

The relationship of the parties also reflects the leverage created by the inherent value of the worker to the system. At Yamaha, workers possess skills that make it difficult to replace them, while in the manufacturing climate of Hitachi workers can be replaced more easily. In a system where there are no links to help share knowledge throughout the organization, employee involvement is often narrowly focused on self-interest and cannot be shifted to consider more common interests.

Thus, both mass production facilities we studied featured various forms of knowledge creation but with relatively little employee involvement. As a result, the knowledge creation was limited. In one case, the lack of employee involvement reflected an adversarial legacy. In the other case, the lack of employee involvement reflected a lack of pressure to change. Neither organization was knowledge driven, and each would have to follow very different paths to become knowledge driven.

Employee Involvement Driving Knowledge Creation within Boundaries

In mass production, knowledge creation is not essential and employee involvement becomes an "add-on" activity. In an STS context, knowledge creation is essential to the optimizing of the sociotechnical balance. In this regard, employees are seen as having unique insights into the quality of their worklives, the safety of their work areas, and the distribution of assignments among team members. To achieve improvements along these dimensions, the involvement of employees is essential.

At the Coil Center, there were high levels of involvement through mechanisms such as job rotation, worker-led quality inspection, and within-team decision making. Workers developed skills and knowledge about the work they performed and the quality of the product. For example, they were trained in how to recognize and prevent defects in the steel products they created.

In addition to the production team, temporary workers handled some of the packaging and warehousing activities. There were also clerical employees in the office area. Relatively little information sharing took place across these groups. In fact, the huge glass wall separating the production workers from the clerical workers was even seen as something of a divide between the two groups. Documents taped up to share information had the opposite effect. Instead of expanding information, they created visual barriers that increased the social distance between people in the two work areas.

To be fair, management at the Coil Center did not set out to be an example of either a sociotechnical system workplace or an example of "Japanese" management practices. We were explicitly told that the goal was to achieve sufficiently high product quality and dependability to succeed as a first-tier supplier. What is interesting is why within-team involvement was seen as essential in achieving this goal but other forms of involvement were not. This is a knowledge-driven work system, but the knowledge is confined within team boundaries and focused on a subset of specific social or technical issues. As a result, these forms of knowledge can drive only a bounded set of improvements.

At I/NTek, the scope of involvement is much broader though still set within team boundaries. The roles and responsibilities of the groups are broader, in part due to the increased scale of the operations. At the time of our visits, teams were still organized by turns or shifts.[13] The teams were responsible for scheduling, production control, and training requests; had a voice in selecting new members to the team; and oversaw a greater than usual degree of budgetary administration.

Given the massive technological investment and the substantial costs of production stoppages, worker knowledge on these issues is critical to a firm's profitability. In addition, workers must constantly be aware of challenges surrounding workplace and environmental safety. Daily operations at I/NTek depend highly on employee involvement.

What form did this involvement take? First, there was an elaborate set of joint governance mechanisms. For example, joint councils focused on concerns in four broad areas: product and plant quality, workplace environment and safety, activities and involvement for team members and their families, and personal/socio policies (i.e., discipline, performance appraisal). The employees on these councils represented a cross-section of the workforce and were not necessarily union representatives. In other words, the councils served as clearinghouses for ideas, information, and projects.

The activities of these councils served to create and distribute knowledge about how to manage potential variation across shifts and work areas in the facility. A risk, however, is that this activity occurs to support itself rather than exist as a direct and continuous extension of a managerial strategic plan. In other words, organizationally focused knowledge may not be shared across all levels (as it often is in lean production settings) due to the internal focus of the STS teams.

Second, there were the traditional forms of off-line employee involvement. The knowledge creation in these cases was focused on team-generated problems, which involved a mix of social and technical topics. Workers were focused on workplace and environmental problems such as rearranging the work area, or, as one person put it, "creature features."

Third, there was great pride in the degree to which people were willing and able to become involved in responding to special circumstances or crises. For example, when there were problems with equipment or when an innovative technique was being tried, workers would answer late-night pages or come in on their own time to help. Workers demonstrated commitment and involvement when they stayed around to see how the situation would work out. The shared knowledge created during these events helped to form different bonds among all the workers and deepened employee commitment to the firm.

Employee Involvement Targeted at Reducing Waste

In a lean manufacturing operation, the tangible signs of involvement are everywhere. Andon boards display real-time information on work operations, while bulletin boards and magnetic boards display work-related information such as task assignments and performance data. Amid the activity of production, there are daily opportunities for people to be involved in quality assessments and problem solving. A lean production site frequently provides spaces adjacent to the work area where workers can meet and interact with each other and where data regarding training, attendance, and workplace details are displayed.[14]

Underlying these tangible indicators is a view of employee involvement that reaches far beyond solving problems or resolving crises. People are involved in work processes not only to deal with an immediate issue but also to build capability for the future. A philosophy exists that rewards fixing the problem rather than assigning blame. Bill Childs, the Vice President of Human Resources for NUMMI, commented in a written statement that he provided to us that "the Toyota Production System, recognized as the most efficient production system in the world, relies heavily on the initiative and cooperation of the individual employee to maintain and improve the day-to-day operations and to achieve continuous improvement in quality and efficiency." He highlighted a set of important underlying assumptions when he also stated, "remember, that even the worst employee will perform the job properly many more times than improperly and it is the positive contributions which must be encouraged and fostered." The focus on employee involvement is not on an occasional idea, but on what happens every day on the job. Credit is assigned to team and individual efforts.[15]

At Denso Manufacturing–Michigan, Inc., the kaizen-teian system categorizes suggestions as "tangible" and "intangible." The company's use of the word "tangible" generally reflects its meaning in this book. It is important to note that "intangible" is used to mean something different from the term as defined in this book. Tangible suggestions are ideas that result in clear dollar savings—those that can be calculated—such as the reduction of a percentage of scrap. Most suggestion systems in traditional U.S. settings emphasize the tangible.

Intangible suggestions, on the other hand, may not be directly linked to immediate dollar savings but are aimed at small, nonmeasurable improvements such as raising a worktable for ergonomic purposes or alphabetizing mailboxes. We were told at Denso Manufacturing–Michigan, Inc., that the intangible suggestions were the most important since they were generally more quickly generated and hence more likely to build the team's capability to make further improvements. People learned how to complete a suggestion form, take it to the appropriate managers and engineers, respond to requests for more data, and other necessary skills.

In fact, one member of our team, Dr. Wen-Jeng Lin, conducted a detailed analysis of the kaizen-teian suggestion system at this location as part of his dissertation research. He constructed a model to test whether the intangible suggestions would predict, over time, the making of tangible suggestions.[16] He found that a firm could increase the number of tangible suggestions by encouraging and implementing the intangible ones. In other words, no improvement is too small.

For example, the president of Denso Manufacturing–Michigan, Inc., made a keynote presentation at the University of Michigan's annual Management Briefing Seminar in 1995. In front of over 1,000 participants and the worldwide automotive media, he and workers from two quality circles shared the stage and told the story behind one of their improvement efforts. It is significant that the firm's leadership chose to share the podium with shop-floor workers. Underlying this event are several crucial points: the people who made the changes were best able to describe their work; the workers demonstrated skills and confidence learned through their successful improvement efforts; and management recognized that knowledge resides in the people who make the improvements.[17]

During this presentation, information was shared at two levels. First, employees presented the actual tangible improvement to the production process of removing waste water from around their machine. Second, part of the presentation was made by shop-floor workers dressed in company uniforms who have the knowledge, skills, and power to make significant changes. Implementation of suggestions not only positively affects the company's profitability, but it also has a positive impact on developing the associates.

At our lean sites, employees generated large numbers of suggestions. Those sites (such as NUMMI, AAI, and Denso Manufacturing–Michigan, Inc.) with kaizen-teian programs had records that indicated that high percentages of the workforce submitted suggestions and that over 90% of these were implemented. Contrast this with the standard mass production attitude in which workers try to submit suggestions that are rewarded with large cash bonuses. Typically, less than half the suggestions submitted are implemented, and employees often wait a long time before they learn if their ideas were acceptable. Both factors discourage further suggestions.

How did the kaizen-teian systems come to look so different from this norm? It did not happen all at once. For example, at NUMMI, the 4,400 hourly workers in the plant submitted a total of 9,767 suggestions in 1994, of which 85.7% were implemented. This is, of course, very impressive. It is important to recognize, however, that in NUMMI's early years a great deal of effort was expended to encourage participation. Even with this effort, the participation level in 1986 was 26%. This grew steadily over the next three or four years until it reached its consistent high levels.

Employee involvement can extend outside the walls of the plant to suppliers or customers. At several organizations, we were told about workers who visit the suppliers to train them in new methods or to discover ways that they could improve their own customer service. For example,

Ogihara workers told about going to Chrysler to learn firsthand about problems with stampings. This information was channeled directly back into the production process to help improve product quality.

Ogihara provides excellent examples of the kinds of relationships that a firm can develop with its customers and others in an industry. They have actually sent production workers from their Japanese headquarters and the Howell plant to Mexico and Sweden to help these facilities improve their existing stamping operations. Knowledge is created, shared, and diffused in these activities. The knowledge base of every organization in this loop is increased by direct employee involvement.

It is important to understand the kaizen dynamics in their cross-cultural context. In a workplace, where notions of involvement and participation from workplaces in one country are being introduced to workplaces in another, the process goes through the additional filters associated with the different cultural meanings associated with these concepts. For example, when we visited the Denso Nishio factory near Nagoya, Japan, we observed an organization in which the processes for participation and the mechanisms for standardization had been honed through nearly three decades of kaizen efforts. In Battle Creek at the Denso Manufacturing–Michigan, Inc., facility, there was the desire to foster the same broad-based input. The company also wanted that input to be effectively aimed at clear improvement objectives.

If Denso Manufacturing–Michigan, Inc., placed too much emphasis on introducing participatory ideas without also introducing the discipline of improvement objectives, then people would feel involved but their knowledge would not necessarily be driving the work system in the most appropriate ways. On the other hand, if the systems were imported "as is" from Japan, it would likely seem overly constraining since there would be no historical context to understand why people spend so much energy making sure that their suggestion-making activity conforms to higher management priorities.

Implications for Employee Power in Knowledge-Driven Work Systems

In either the lean or STS work systems, employee involvement leads to increasing capability on the part of workers. The intended focus of this capability is different under the two systems: one optimizes the reduction of waste and the other optimizes the balance between social and technical aspects of worklife. Inevitably, there are also unintended consequences of increased employee capabilities. In particular, as employees become more capable of surfacing and solving problems there are implications for parties who traditionally see it as their responsibility to solve these problems.

Examining the relationship between employees in a knowledge-driven work system and the unions representing these employees can help one understand the implications of these new capabilities. Our interest here is in unions as formal institutions and in unions in a broader sense—as the embodiment of collective interests and community within a work-force. Issues that we surface in this analysis are extended in the chapter on labor relations.

Throughout their history, unions have always sought to increase employee voice in the workplace. For example, the preamble to the UAW constitution states, "The workers must have a voice in their own destiny and the right to participate in making decisions that affect their lives before such decisions are made."[18] In this respect, it would seem that increasingly knowledge-driven workplaces would be deeply valued by unions. In fact, as we visited the unionized facilities that were also knowledge driven, we did meet many union leaders who spoke with great pride about the problem-solving accomplishments of their members. For example, the president of the Steelworkers local that represents the workers at both I/NTek and I/N Kote, spoke with enthusiasm about the way workers solved the crisis around the broken rollers. We also met many union members who saw their unions as instrumental in establishing key aspects of their work systems.

However, there is much more to this picture. This is a clear case in which details matter. Even if unions value knowledge and involvement in principle, the specific challenges arise around the daily roles of elected and appointed union representatives. A union steward who defined her role around solving problems that employees have with seemingly inappropriate demands by management will find that employees are now solving many of these problems. Other problems may be less common since managers are increasingly attentive to employees who are now the primary source of quality inspection, job assignments, and other daily tasks. At a fundamental level, a key aspiration of the union has been achieved—but as a result of the production system rather than of specific collective actions.

Although people are more empowered with respect to daily decisions, the power that they now have is very complicated. Particularly in the lean operations, the removal of buffers makes the system much more dependent on the voluntary commitment and extra effort of employees. Yet employees are also much less likely to abuse this power since they are more aware of the needs and pressures from internal and external customers. Thus, union power is derived less from the threat to withhold labor.

Furthermore, as employees become more knowledgeable their priorities expand to include larger strategic issues that are traditionally reserved as management rights or the domain of leadership experts. These include issues such as investment in new technology, movement of work in and out of facilities, and environmental procedures.

So what is the nature of a union in such a workplace? The common ties for workers are not as much their opposition to management as their expanded capabilities and their broader horizons. This may still place employees and managers in conflict, but it also involves them in many areas of common concern.

Thus, the capabilities that derive from increased employee involvement in a knowledge-driven work system pose fundamental questions for unions. These questions begin with unions as formal institutions and extend to their broader roles as sources of community in a workplace and as the embodiment in society of an adversarial relationship with management.

Conclusion

We began this chapter by discussing four dilemmas. First, there was the dilemma centering on managers' need for involvement but their desire for control. We have seen that the need for control and accountability is the product of operating in a system that is set up to be driven by top-down expert knowledge. Where people are involved in operations that are knowledge driven, there is less need for traditional forms of top-down control. In fact, exercising these types of control would undermine operations. There is still a need—even a greater need—for coordination at higher levels, but the priority is as much for coordination on intangibles such as values and mission as it is on tangible outcomes.

The second dilemma centered on individual leaders or parts of the organization succeeding at the expense of others—optimizing parts of the system rather than the whole. We have seen that the broad base of increased capability achieved through knowledge-driven involvement serves to increase awareness of interdependence, to reduce the importance of status differences, to highlight the value of experiential learning, and to increase the credibility of nontraditional sources of knowledge. At the same time, there are fewer chances to blame others, shirk responsibility, or focus only on superficial symptoms of deeper problems.

The third dilemma centered on the short-term focus that prevails in traditional work systems. We have seen that a knowledge-driven work system depends on a long-term focus on investment in employee capability. Kaizen capability—as some organizations use the term—is built over time. For example, at NUMMI the initial numbers of suggestions implemented were small but increased substantially as the workforce became more capable with the kaizen process. The reason this takes a long time is that the increased capability is needed on intangible aspects of operations, such as valuing experience and knowledge.

In this context, what is often seen in a traditional workplace as a lack of appreciation for employee capabilities or as little "follow-up" on group suggestions may actually reflect a lack of understanding or even awareness of deeper system issues. It is easy in hindsight to be critical of managers for not seeing the larger system, but they typically operate in a world that is centered on applying quick fixes. The dominant mindset is, "if it ain't broke, don't fix it." Only in the face of severe competitive pressures on issues of quality, cost, and customer service has it been possible to consider that there may be fundamental flaws in the system.

Today, many managers and workers have concluded that fundamental changes in workplaces are essential. As a result, change centered on systems, organizations, and teams has drawn a great deal of attention.[19] Managers have sought to apply a systems approach through an emphasis on technical innovations such as statistical process control, JIT delivery, flow-through manufacturing, and simultaneous engineering. Unfortunately, many of these innovations are implemented using a piecemeal strategy. Even where many of the innovations are implemented at the same time, they are not typically integrated into an overall system.

One aspect of the organizations we studied was the presence of Japanese partners who had an organizational and cultural base that supported the long-term horizon and a systems focus. This is one aspect of the diffusion process that has greatly facilitated the introduction of knowledge-driven work systems. It is much harder to make such a shift in an existing organization where there is no well-defined internal group advocating for the alternative approach in a coordinated way.

Finally, there is the enduring dilemma concerning the importance of standardization and the need for diverse inputs. A knowledge-driven work system will rise or fall on the attention to this dilemma. The strength of such a system lies in its enormous capacity for providing much new input of knowledge and expertise. At the same time, if there are no strong mechanisms to channel and coordinate the input, the system risks becoming overloaded. In this regard, we observed organizations placing a great premium on clear overarching goals. We also observed well-defined boundaries at the shop-floor level within which a great deal of improvement energy was encouraged—so long as it stayed within those boundaries. Over time, the overarching goals and the shop-floor boundaries may evolve—based on learning from experience—but the need for these mechanisms is continuing.

Thus, knowledge-driven work systems—especially in the context of global diffusion—help to resolve many traditional managerial dilemmas. At the same time, these emerging forms of employee involvement create new challenges.

6

Constructing
Employment Security
· ·

Understanding the Emergence
of Mutual Commitment

E mployment security represents a central but little understood foundation for work teams, kaizen, and virtual knowledge. For the most
part, however, public attention has centered on specific employment
security guarantees (such as no-layoff clauses) rather than on the complex mix of practices and processes that together make such a policy possible. The focus of this chapter is on linkages between employment security and knowledge-driven work systems.[1]

The issue of employment security is complicated. For at least a half
dozen years, the business press in the United States has documented the
collapse of social contracts between employers and employees. Workers
and managers alike are urged to build their own portable skill set and
take personal responsibility for their career survival and development.
In this context, discussion of employment security seems almost a throw-
back to an earlier era. In fact, it is the context of a deteriorating social
contract that makes the issue so interesting and important. We observed
employers, unions, and workers who were coming to value their investments in knowledge and capability. As a result, they were attempting to
piece together some semblance of guarantees, assurances, or at least
understandings that would support this process—despite the reverse
direction of practices in the larger society.

Employment security has the potential to alter the basic assumptions
that underlie an employment relationship. This occurs where it is properly managed and successfully integrated into a larger workplace system.

Essential management considerations include day-to-day techniques such as proper scheduling of overtime, use of temporaries and contract workers, multiskilling, as well as flexible assignment of work. The integration of an employment security policy calls for a tempering or realigning of traditional tactics and attitudes. For example, employment security drives reciprocal understandings in which management and workers share a fair portion of the benefits of growth as well as the challenges of economic hardship.

Unless employment security is an integral component of the employment relationship, its impact will be limited. At best, it becomes just one part of a calculable trade-off in a compensation package. Inevitably, it requires a significant departure from the traditional employment security approach based on a job control and seniority system. The shift from negotiated benefit to integrated policy requires all those involved to reassess the entire structure of the employment relations bargain as well as the values they have traditionally assigned to individual elements of the employment relationship.

Employment security—manifest as what some people term "lifetime" employment practices—is frequently seen as a distinct feature of the Japanese economy.[2] In fact, even in Japan the principle applies only to the portion of the workforce employed by larger corporations. Today, there are tensions and possible changes occurring in these practices in Japan.[3] Still, this system rests on assumptions that are often seen as distinctly Japanese, such as enterprise unionism and the seniority wage system.[4] Large-scale intra-firm transfers, temporary and permanent transfers to affiliated firms, and even non-affiliated firms were essential elements of this strategy. Companies later established structures that enabled them to transfer workers more frequently in an effort to respond flexibly to short- and long-term changes in production volume. This raises core issues around the transferability of these practices to the U.S. context.[5]

In the United States, unlike Japan, there is not a parallel set of institutional arrangements supporting employment security. In fact, most employees are considered employees at will under the law, which means that they can even be fired without just cause. In recent years, the massive layoffs of white-collar and blue-collar employees have led many observers to proclaim the end of any social contracts that did exist.[6] Under the rubric of reengineering, "right-sizing," or restructuring, these layoffs are prompting individuals to look out for their own careers and employment.[7] Still, there are employers, including some of the organizations we studied, who do provide a significant measure of employment security.

To assure meaningful employment security in the United States, companies must provide more than just written guarantees. Given the present context, people will be skeptical even of a written guarantee or policy. For people to demonstrate commitment, companies must pay attention to the intangibles, especially with respect to the way employment security policies support other aspects of daily operations.

For example, lean production is not a fixed, technical work system. When it works, it is virtually a living organization that is constantly creating itself. In this context, lean production depends on kaizen and other people-driven processes for continuous improvement. Kaizen, in turn, depends on sustained employee commitment combined with a stable foundation of shared knowledge. Employment security becomes a centerpiece of lean production, not for benevolent reasons but because it is so central to reinforcing commitment and preserving investment in human capital.[8]

Defining Employment Security in Practice

Based on our observations, we define employment security as a set of unique, internal understandings regarding employees' and employers' mutual responsibilities for the continuity of work and employee commitment. The construction of these understandings may be driven by either party. This could be the employer, the employees, or representatives serving either.

However driven, employment security redirects attention from the external labor market to the internal labor market. The focus is on increased human capital investment by both the employer and the employees. In this respect, pursuing employment security represents a core business strategy.

At Denso Manufacturing–Michigan, Inc., employees improve their workplace through thousands of individual suggestions that have as their ultimate goal the continued competitive improvement of the firm.[9] These suggestions are not considered separate, individual events. They all employ common processes and build upon one another. Through accumulated kaizen efforts and technical training, the expertise and skills of workers increase over time.

Without valuing and utilizing this expertise, processes that are essential elements of new production systems cannot function. For example, job rotation within work teams is impossible unless team members have acquired and are encouraged to utilize multiple skills. Effective kaizen or continuous improvement that relies on small incremental changes requires the consistent presence of an employee or team. Workers feel secure about their continued employment when they know they are central to business success. Employers must be clear about this linkage and respond through formal or informal processes to maintain employment security.

With increased employment security, an environment can develop in which workers begin to take greater risks and assume more responsibility through participatory programs. For example, increased employment security provided a critical foundation for the agreement at I/NTek to reduce job classifications and to share traditional managerial tasks such as budgeting and scheduling. The number of job classifications can be reduced as workers conclude that they no longer need these protections against arbitrary managerial decisions. At the same time, managers will grant these guarantees when flexibility and worker commitment are priorities.

All eight of our sites have had to confront employee concerns about employment security. This is even an issue in the first-wave sites, which generally follow traditional U.S. patterns of employment practices. There is a wide range of responses to this issue. In some cases, the response involves a management practice of seeking to avoid layoffs. Avoiding layoffs can be achieved through reductions in overtime, reduced use of temporary workers, and reassignment of workers to nontraditional jobs (such as training or customer relations or facility maintenance). We observed a response along these lines at Yamaha Musical Products, one of our first-wave sites, as well as at all of the second-wave sites. For example, the senior Japanese manager at Yamaha Musical Products, "Steve" Hara, stated, "The first question that comes up when business is slow is 'when will the layoff come?' I always say that it is the last thing we will do. It is our responsibility to maintain stable employment."

It is also possible for layoff avoidance language to be embodied in union contracts or employee policy handbooks. Finally, where a full range of practices aimed at fostering employment security is in place, a strong "social contract" or shared set of understandings between employees and the employer may emerge.[10] The presence or absence of a union does not limit this full range of practices and the possible emergence of a social contract.

There is one very important feature of any employment security practice. The assurances, whether specified in a contract or built into management practice, do not have shared social meaning until the parties face a test event. These events are situations in which a layoff would normally have occurred and, instead, alternative practices are employed. In a very real sense, these are pivotal events. The employment security assurances are either reinforced or undercut by the response to the situation. Where the assurances are reinforced, a stronger social contract is forged.

For example, the startup phase at the Coil Center extended through December 1991—a time when an economic downturn led its major customers to cut back on their production schedules and arrange extended plant shutdowns during the holidays. Since there was an 11-day period of no demand for its products, the Coil Center could have laid off its employees. In fact, the employees received full pay during this time for 10 of the 11 days. They spent time in the plant in training, maintenance, and other activities. The company wanted to be able to respond to any new orders if they were to arrive during this period. Ultimately, when all the customers were shut down, the employees were given longer vacations. This management decision during the early stages of the operation was pivotal. It reinforced the company's assurances of avoiding layoffs and helped to increase employee commitment to the firm.

Broadly speaking, the range of employment security practices can be classified into three categories or dimensions. First, there is a set of informal practices associated with avoiding layoffs; these can be modest in scope or very aggressive. Second, there is a set of formal policies that can be embodied in a contract or policy manual; these can also vary from relatively modest assurances to very strong language. Finally, there is a set of reciprocal understandings that are part of what we are terming "social contracts" linked to worker commitment. We see these as embedded dimensions since formal policies and social contracts almost always rest on a mix of concurrent informal practices. Table 6.1 classifies our eight sites across these three dimensions.

As table 6.1 suggests, there is a clear distinction between the first- and second-wave sites. In the first-wave sites, we see only informal no-layoff practices. In contrast, all but one of the second-wave sites feature a more extensive mix of tactics. The second-wave unionized sites are all consistent in having contract language that directly addresses the issue of employment security, but one of these sites does not feature a reciprocal social contract linked to worker commitment. None of the second-wave nonunion sites had formal employment security policies, although two featured reciprocal social contracts linked to worker commitment. Given these findings, it is important to examine more closely the meaning of employment security across unionized and nonunionized sites.

Employment Security Practices in Unionized and Nonunionized Sites

The most explicit treatments of the employment security issue can be found in three of our five unionized sites—AAI, NUMMI, and I/NTek. The contract language in all three cases follows along similar lines. The UAW–AAI contract language, for example, outlines specific, extreme circumstances under which a layoff might occur. Further, the contract

Table 6.1 Research Sites Classified by Employment Security Practices

		Three dimensions of employment security*		
	Research sites	Informal no-layoff practice	Formal employment security policy or contract language	Reciprocal social contracts linked to worker commitment
First wave, union	Hitachi Magnetics	X		
	Yamaha Musical Products	X		
Second wave, nonunion	Coil Center	X		
	Denso Manufacturing–Michigan, Inc.	X		X
	Ogihara	X		X
Second wave, union	AAI	X	X	
	I/NTek	X	X	X
	NUMMI	X	X	X

*"Informal no-layoff practice" means either that there are instances where market conditions would have suggested a layoff in a traditional organization but no one was in fact laid off or that the business is managed in such a way that there is no expectation of laying off employees. "Formal employment security policy or contract language" refers to explicit contractual assurances or policies that limit the likelihood of job loss. "Reciprocal social contracts linked to worker commitment" reflect a situation in which workers voluntarily contribute their knowledge and effort in support of continuous improvement with the understanding that they will not be disadvantaged and that every effort will be made to maintain continuity of employment.

articulates a philosophy in which the centrality of employment security is recognized. The specific language reads as follows:

> In general, AAI recognizes the critical importance of job security to the well being of its employees, their attitudes towards and their efforts on behalf of the company. The company also acknowledges that the cooperation and contribution of its employees are crucially important to its ability to compete in the U.S. auto market. Moreover, the company recognizes its basic responsibility, both to its employees and the communities in which it operates, to provide stable and secure employment to the fullest extent possible.
>
> For all of these reasons, AAI agrees that it will not lay off employees unless compelled to do so by economic conditions and financial circumstances so severe that its long-term financial viability is threatened. Even then, the company will take affirmative measures before instituting any layoffs, including but not limited to such action as: the reduction of salaries of its officers and management, and other jointly determined cost cutting measures, insourcing work previously contracted out; the utilization of bargaining unit employees in training programs, quality and customer satisfaction teams; and other non-traditional work assignments. Should layoffs ever be un-

avoidable, a jointly developed, mutually satisfactory program will be implemented that provides layoffs and recalls will be in accordance with seniority and provides the opportunity for voluntary layoffs. In the final analysis, both parties agree that job security and the company's ability to compete and prosper are inseparably linked one to the other.

Additionally, in the UAW–AAI system, there is the following guarantee for compensable time off:

> Seniority employees will be compensated for 80 percent of the total of their base rate plus the present cost-of-living allowance for the regular straight time hours not worked due to company mandated time off as: part shortage, equipment breakdown, act of God or due to market turndown in sales. Compensation received by an employee within this provision will not exceed seventy consecutive weeks.[11]

Altogether, the AAI language represents a set of very strong assurances to employees regarding the employer's commitment to avoid layoffs and provide income continuity. The UAW–NUMMI contract also guarantees employment unless decline in demand is so severe that it threatens the long-term viability of the company. Before any layoffs occur at NUMMI, the top 65 management personnel will take a salary cut and jobs currently contracted out will be brought back into the plant. Similarly, at I/NTek the contractual agreement provides that the facility will not be shut down except in a catastrophic economic disaster and layoffs will not take place until after there have been reductions in hours and other adjustments. Special income guarantees are also provided for the high-seniority (highly skilled) employees who transferred into the facility from Inland Steel. These guarantees provide for up to one year of pay at full wage rates regardless of their reassignment to lower-paying positions. Material handlers were paid approximately $8–10 an hour while operators were paid at $12–15 an hour. The material handlers, mechanics, and others who did not transfer from Inland do not have this guarantee, but they do have the assurances on avoiding layoffs that are in the union contract. Thus, the union contracts contain a distinction between assurances that layoffs will be avoided and guarantees of income during periods of adversity.

The two remaining unionized sites do not have contractual assurances or income guarantees on these issues.[12] In fact, the language on layoffs and seniority in these contracts is quite similar to most U.S. union contracts, providing for seniority progression within specified job classifications. The contracts are written to support a system in which layoffs are common responses to fluctuations in product demand. In the case of Hitachi, that is exactly how the contract was administered for many years.

At Yamaha Musical Products, however, there is much greater attention to avoiding layoffs, despite the lack of formal contract language. In response to a question as to whether or not Yamaha Musical Products would lay people off, if business were slow, the executive vice president and the personnel director both responded that "we would try not to" but "we can't guarantee this." They indicated that they would do this "only as a last resort." In fact, the only major layoff at Yamaha in the past 25 years has been during the period when the original facility was being shut down and work was being transferred to the new facility a few miles away.

The chair of the union bargaining committee confirmed this view, stating that he believes there is an implicit policy of no layoffs. Layoffs that occur are generally of a temporary nature and very rare. He stated that there is a belief that the Japanese style of management is at odds with the concept of layoffs. He indicated that this has increased feelings of employment security and was convinced that people would not be terminated without "real justification." Thus, while there is no contract language at Yamaha Musical Products comparable to that of NUMMI, AAI, or I/NTek, there is a similar end result—no layoffs.

Interestingly, early in the relationship between Yamaha Musical Products and the UAW, the union did seek formal contract language on employment security. At the time, the company indicated that its commitment to no-layoff practices remained strong, but it chose not to agree to formal contract language. In fact, subsequent practices have confirmed the company's commitment. It is interesting to reflect on what the outcome of such discussion would have been had these negotiations occurred after NUMMI and some of the other companies and their unions had included formal policies in their contracts. It is likely that both labor and management in the first-wave sites did not have a frame of reference in which they could fully understand the mutual commitments that we now understand to be a part of employment security.

Among the nonunion sites, there is a common commitment to follow a similar mix of practices as alternatives to layoffs. While these sites do not feature formal policy provisions that rival the AAI, NUMMI, and I/NTek contracts, the practices seem to be at least as aggressive in avoiding layoffs. Companies that wish to remain nonunion must abide by the implicit guarantees of their social contracts. Their workers perceive employment security to be a trade-off for higher wages and greater scheduling flexibility. This commitment has been stated explicitly in a variety of interviews with workers at both union and nonunion plants. For example, a manager at Ogihara commented, "there is a high degree of faith and trust in management. There is an informal social contract tied to trust. Employees have invested a high level of confidence in management." Despite the high levels of confidence in a number of our nonunionized sites, there was also an undercurrent of caution around just how strong the employment security assurances were. This was described by a number of individuals as "waiting for the other shoe to drop." Over time, and after various test events, the concern over "the other shoe" did seem to diminish. This represents a gradual movement away from the set of beliefs and assumptions that are dominant in most U.S. workforces.

Ogihara has avoided layoffs using these methods, as well as carefully hiring and staffing with temporary employees who can be released on short notice to protect the regular workforce. No written guarantee exists, but there is an implied lifetime guarantee of a job. Charlotte Aimer, facilitator, told us, "I have the greatest respect for T. Ogihara. He sees us as a family and worries about poor economic times. People are secure here; it's not written, just informal." Another facilitator, Tobey Miller, echoed these sentiments when he said that T. Ogihara and the Ogihara executives "do not believe in layoffs, and I have real faith in that."

A business downturn in the auto industry was the cause of a serious crisis at NUMMI. Sales of the Nova dropped radically in 1988. This provided a test of contract language that guaranteed the workers employment security unless there was a significant financial threat to the survival of the company. While a new model was being introduced into the factory, workers were sent through a one-week training course, 250 at a time. The training program was designed, developed, and taught by bargaining-unit employees to meet specific training needs that production workers identified. This experience also exemplifies the idea that the firm is actually developing a "body" of operating knowledge and expertise in the workforce.

At Denso Manufacturing–Michigan, Inc., the senior vice president for administration, Stan Tooley, explained the firm's position on employment security. He related a story about the company's president, who publicly announced that if one worker were laid off he would be the first to leave. Mike Gagnon, manager of organizational development, stressed the positive aspects of Denso Manufacturing–Michigan, Inc.'s philosophy of employment security when he reported,

> You don't face psychological consequences of looking for work. In slow times, associates will be used in useful activities. In times of slow down, a coordinated effort will be initiated—a morale survey could

be done and associates would be involved in problem-solving activities. Job security builds trust, loyalty, and commitment.

Clearly, this is not just about a no-layoff clause or a long-term employment practice. Workers who begin to have a much deeper relationship with their employers are in the process of creating a new mutually beneficial reality in their workplaces. The reciprocal nature of these relationships is for many workers tentative and still forming. It is different from the previous long spans of unbroken employment that many American workers experienced 40 years ago. During that period, buffers, prosperity, and the traditions of a mass production economy helped to insulate many workers with a long unbroken employment relationship. At our sites, "employment security" is a term that has begun to define a deepening and shifting relationship that is being articulated by each individual employer and workforce out of their shared experiences.

Workers have a deeply held set of standards for equitable behavior. If these standards are upheld, the trust between a firm and its workers remains intact despite reductions in workforce. This is illustrated by the techniques used in many joint ventures to maintain employment security for the regular workforce—techniques such as flexible use of overtime, temporary workers, and contract labor. For example, workers understand the relationship between greater use of mandatory overtime as opposed to hiring additional employees that might then be laid off if business fluctuates. However, the use of temporary workers introduces a new tension in the workplace among permanent workers. While employment security reinforces a sense of fairness, a parallel dependence on temporary workers diminishes it.

Across the unionized and nonunionized sites, there are notable differences in employment security practices—particularly concerning the degree to which no-layoff assurances are recorded as written policies. However, at a more fundamental level the emergent and reciprocal nature of employment security cuts across all sites.

Linking Employment Security to the Production System

To what degree does the nature of a production system influence the provision of employment security assurances? In our sites, we highlight three distinct systems for employee involvement that are linked to alternative production systems. These systems are (1) lean production with a distinct form of highly interdependent teams, (2) continuous process production linked to STS teams, and (3) mass production linked to off-line teams. We will examine employment security in each of these contexts.

The shift to lean production requires more than a physical change in the working environment. It is not just the establishment of JIT delivery or the use of reduced in-process inventory or investment in new technology. Lean production represents a business strategy in which quality and continuous improvement are seen as sources of competitive advantage. Employment security is integral to the strategy in the way it drives kaizen.

Kaizen depends on the tangible and intangible skills and knowledge that employees build by virtue of time spent on the job. The differences in strategies are vividly illustrated by the different workplace practices followed at NUMMI compared with those at the previous GM Fremont facility. At Fremont, layoffs were a common event—tied to ebbs and flows in the automotive marketplace. By contrast, NUMMI has not yet laid off employees since it began operations in 1984. During this time, the market has been no less volatile. In fact, one NUMMI product—the Chevrolet Nova—saw a precipitous decline in sales before a replacement product was found. As we saw earlier, the Nova workers were not laid off. Instead, teams of trainers were trained and classes were held on a wide range of technical and developmental skills. This training has greatly facilitated the subsequent introduction of new products into the plant.

Where sociotechnical systems teams are utilized, employment security is also an essential building block but for different reasons than we saw in the case of lean production. Sociotechnical systems teams take on increasing responsibility for a wide range of managerial functions, typically including work assignments, materials ordering, scheduling of production runs, team-member selection, and even external customer relations. When these core operating functions reside in the hands of line operators, employment security plays two critical functions. First, it would be hard for the operation to function in the absence of these people, given their increased responsibility for traditional managerial tasks. Second, it is unlikely that employees and the union would willingly take on these responsibilities in the absence of such assurance. In fact, if there were the sort of turnover that characterizes a system in which layoffs are not uncommon, there would be neither the capability nor the willingness to handle these operational tasks.

At I/NTek, employment security has not been a problem as it is at the older Indiana Harbor Inland Steel Plant. Contract language negotiated with the United Steel Workers of America (USWA) states that there will be no layoffs except under "catastrophic" conditions. In reality, the plant's success is relatively secure because Inland Steel sends orders to I/NTek first, due to its low-cost, high-quality product. A level of employment security is inherent in product cost and quality and market acceptance. The initial group of workers, who transferred to I/NTek from Inland, had an average of 15 to 18 years of seniority. They were highly skilled and were relatively secure at Inland, so I/NTek had to provide employment guarantees to attract them away. In the event of economic catastrophe, these original senior people would be allowed to return to Inland as operators with saved rates of pay for one year. Prior to that action, however, the work week in the I/NTek plant would be reduced to 32 hours and material handlers would be laid off. The wage reduction would be substantial if the arrangement lasted over a year. Material handlers make between $8 and $10 an hour, while skilled operators earn $12 to $15 an hour. The theory has not been tested. It raises sensitive issues due to the existence of contract language at other firms that provides for "bumping" senior employees back into other work areas at the expense of less senior workers. Local 1010 members cannot "bump" into the I/NTek facility.[13]

The concerns at I/NTek illustrate the traditional use of layoffs to control staffing levels during periods of economic downturn. The firms in our study that have experienced layoffs are the first-wave firms. The second-wave firms had not yet faced this issue because they were new and growing. Economic downturns at these sites are met with implicit guarantees against layoffs and strenuous efforts to avoid any adverse impact on the workers. Firms often use training or reassignment of duties to bridge the space more commonly filled by a layoff in U.S. firms.

One major distinction that affects the type of response that may be used is the presence of a collective bargaining agreement. Contract language is meant to dictate how firms should treat their workers and to protect union members from arbitrary action. Rules are necessary and negotiated for the use of overtime, temporary and contract workers, and layoffs. These traditional influences are seen in contracts in the older first-wave sites. All these techniques are seniority based and have traditionally offered few alternatives.

Daily operations at I/NTek provide a view of how alternatives may be implemented. For example, the work teams essentially run the plant. This includes daily decisions on all aspects of operations and even such sensitive issues as the early problem solving in a situation that could ultimately lead to discipline. Management "resources" originally provided technical assistance to the teams. However, the range of tasks involving technical assistance by these managers has become very limited. The amount of assistance they can provide is restricted, partly because of the high level of work-specific knowledge that resides within a given team.[14]

Even with the core functional role that teams play in the I/NTek system, the administration of employment security contract language has been an iterative learning process. Consider the lessons that emerged from a pivotal event that occurred relatively early in plant operations. The plant faced a crisis when it discovered a supplier defect in all 40 of the rollers used in the final rolling line as well as in all of the back-up rollers. These rollers are custom made, and it was estimated that it would take two to three months for replacement rollers to be fabricated, thus idling more than half of the workforce in the facility. There was no question that this circumstance fully met with the contractual definition of a catastrophic event, and the instant response from corporate headquarters was to initiate the process for layoffs. It was the response at the plant that indicates the way an employment security practice must rest on actual experience.

The local union and management responded with a request to utilize the flexibility and the capabilities built into the contract around managing employment security. Top management called on the plant to demonstrate that such an approach would be both feasible and cost-effective. The local union leaders then circulated among employees in the plant to build the case for being proactive and not just taking a layoff with income protections, which might seem to be an easier option. Local union and management leaders jointly called together the employees who were directly involved. These employees brainstormed a variety of ways that they might be able to add value while the rollers were being fixed. These options included taking on some preventive maintenance work, taking over some work being handled by outside contractors, and other activities. This caused the displacement of some temporary workers. The employees developed an integrated response that met top management's demand that it be both feasible and cost-effective. Interestingly, one engineer went home and constructed a prototype model for a temporary repair that could be completed in one to two months. The plan turned out to be viable. Thus, the idle period was not quite as long as anticipated, and the capabilities embodied in the contract were fully realized.

There are many lessons to be drawn from this incident. First, we see that senior U.S. managers operating in the context of an employment security system do not automatically change their instinctive responses to a crisis just by virtue of being in such a system. Second, a viable response required proactive work by the local union, plant management, and the employees. In the short term, administering a layoff would have been easier for all concerned, but it would not have built long-term capability in the system to handle future crises, and it might have undercut the emerging social contract. Third, key information necessary for a viable response resided in a broad mix of stakeholders, which meant that a decision-making process was required that involved using the skills, experience, and knowledge of all these parties in responding to the crisis. Thus, we see that in an advanced STS setting employment security is central to business operations but that it is also a set of understandings that takes on full meaning only during actual shared experiences.

In traditional mass production or batch production operations, employment security is not a functional requirement. These systems do not depend on the free flow of ideas that is essential to kaizen, nor do they depend on the broad range of operational responsibilities associated with STS. Still, in our traditional sites we find evidence for significant attention to informal employment security practices.

For example, at Yamaha Musical Products the only layoffs were associated with the construction of a new plant. The practice of avoiding layoffs is consistent with Yamaha Musical Products' business strategy of focusing on high-quality products and with the craft skills associated with the assembly of musical instruments. Note, however, that seniority-based job movement is a point of tension in the system precisely because the bidding and "bumping" is driven by an interest in protecting individual rights. This creates a dilemma because the work at Yamaha is much more knowledge driven than in the typical mass production setting. In this case, informal employment security practices help sustain individual commitment, but they are not linked to building shared knowledge or mutual commitments in the organization.

At Hitachi Magnetics, only one clerical employee had been laid off in the years prior to our visits.[15] Reciprocal understandings around mutual commitment are difficult to forge. There are also points of tension in this system. For example, a Japanese manager commented:

> The employment security system is influenced by Japanese practice. We don't do as much layoff and discharge because we are Japanese. We should do more for our profit position. You need a mixture of U.S. and Japanese thinking. We need more severe action. We must decrease our fixed costs and therefore we need to decrease people. I am thinking U.S. because I am in the U.S. Many people are thinking Japanese. I think we need more American thinking.

Thus, the issue of employment security is clearly on the agenda at Hitachi Magnetics, but there is open debate over just how strong the assurances should be.

Ironically, the human resource practices put in place to moderate staffing during business downturns have a different impact within a contemporary framework such as lean production. In lean production, staffing control techniques are used to prevent the layoffs of highly trained and valued employees. This reflects a change in assumptions that is fundamentally different in mass production. United States companies have hired new workers when business was growing and fired or laid off these workers after the boom. In good economic times, displaced workers were able to move to other jobs. The costs to the firm, whether financial, social, or intellectual (in terms of lost tacit knowledge), were not considered.

In today's "borderless economy," the value of employment security for workers increases as firms downsize or relocate to remain competitive.[16] At the firms we visited, especially the nonunion firms, workers understood how this cycle of hiring and firing worked. The use of contract and temporary workers protected them; however, they were at best ambivalent about the equity issues. In second-wave sites, we observed the following differences: more cross-training of workers to facilitate job rotation, a greater emphasis on social-contract implementation skills such as active listening, conflict resolution, group problem solving, and greater sharing of information concerning the business strategy and the financial health of the firm. When employees are involved in the firm, they are viewed as an asset instead of a cost that should be reduced.[17]

This change in viewing workers as an asset instead of a cost is anchored in the increasingly competitive economic environment. Lean or STS production companies that are team based are well prepared to utilize the accumulated knowledge of the workforce. If a stable workforce is essential to this knowledge base, then employment security is a cornerstone to the success of the system.[18] Therefore, in all our sites there were implicit and explicit guarantees of employment security. The tactics to achieve a greater level of employment security varied according to union status and the wave of investment.

The employment security guarantees prevalent in Japanese transplants today owe their roots to the Japanese-style employment system. The Japanese-style employment or lifetime employment policy was developed after World War II in Japan before Japanese labor unions were fully legitimized.[19] As Yang observed, Japanese-style employment was one of the building blocks for the development of the lean production system.

> The success of Japanese firms in the past 20 years shows that stable employment and team-oriented human resource management policies have become the prerequisite on which the success of new production technologies in terms of flexible production, process-based quality control, team work and JIT inventory strategies depend.[20]

The Japanese-style employment system could not be copied directly from Japan since parts of the system, such as seniority pay based on the number of a worker's dependents, are clearly illegal in the United States.

Hence, only parts of the Japanese-style employment system were adopted in order to provide the economic benefits that a stable long-term employment system can yield.

Another important difference that is observable between the Japanese-style employment system and the U.S. system is the self-identification of Japanese workers to the companies they work for instead of to their jobs. American workers have traditionally identified themselves by their trade or occupation as opposed to the company for which they work. Many of the sites we visited made attempts to establish a sense of company identification or culture in order to promote equity and common interests. Areas of common interests were used to break down barriers between workers and managers and among workers themselves. At NUMMI and Denso Manufacturing–Michigan, Inc., methods used to foster a sense of community included having all employees wear identical uniforms, avoiding reserved parking spots, and building a common cafeteria for management and workers. These practices stand in stark contrast to traditional U.S. practices and policies that often intentionally erect barriers between the management and hourly employees.

The observed practices regarding employment security at our sites resulted in a number of changes in the expectations of the workforce. Employment security allowed workers to participate more willingly in their workplace. Mike Hoffman, union chairperson at Yamaha's UAW local, stated that Yamaha's employment security provisions have "given employees latitude to fit in a niche where they can be happy. The company goes to great lengths to find slots for people."

We have seen that employment security is functionally required in lean and STS settings but for different reasons. In the case of lean production, the assurances serve to sustain continuous improvements. In the STS cases, employment security underpins the functional autonomy of teams. In traditional settings, employment security is also helpful in addressing such issues as quality, preventive maintenance, and employee involvement. Since work in these settings is still organized around individual jobs, however, employment security practices are not functionally required in the same way as in the lean and STS cases. Thus, employment security takes on very different meanings, depending on the way work is organized. In systems that rely on shared knowledge among workers, it becomes a central feature.

Who Is at Risk?

We have already seen that employment security is not just something that an employer does or doesn't grant. It is a much more complicated concept. Still, the attempt to provide some group of employees with a measure of employment security does not assure the same degree of security for all employees. Indeed, guarantees for some may even increase the risk for others. To fully understand the nature and dynamics of employment security, one should examine who is at risk of losing their jobs across our various work sites.

In the lean production settings, the most immediately apparent risk would arise due to the application of kaizen principles. An emphasis on reducing waste and on continuous improvement will point to countless process improvements in which fewer people will be required to accomplish the same amount of work. For kaizen to reach its ultimate potential for cost-cutting, effective business strategy must motivate workers to apply their knowledge to continuous improvement. The utilization of strong employment security practices in these settings is required to sustain the kaizen efforts.

However, we have seen that not all employees in these settings are provided with such assurances. In particular, all of our lean production sites employ part-time or temporary workers. Sometimes these people work in support functions (such as cleaning and facility maintenance), while others may be employed in direct production or in technical jobs such as engineering design. For example, when we began our research at Ogihara, there were 390 core employees and a range of 50 to 100 temporary workers—a ratio of 10% to 20% of the total workforce.[21] All of these employees are at much greater risk of job loss during an economic downturn or if needs in the plant shift.

First-line supervisors are commonly seen as being at risk in a team-based setting, but we do not see these people being at risk in the lean production team settings. Instead, the lean system relies on coordination across highly interdependent teams, which in turn involves large numbers of first-line supervisors. For example, at the NUMMI plant the average team has five employees. A first-line supervisor (termed a "coordinator" in that plant) will have responsibility for an average of five teams. This employee-to-supervisor ratio of 25:1 may be a slightly broader span of control than in some organizations, but it still calls for a large number of supervisors. At Denso Manufacturing–Michigan, Inc., the ratio is even smaller—about 15:1. Despite the popular notion that team-based work systems will mean a reduction in the number of supervisors, it really means a change in their roles rather than a change in their numbers.

In the case of the STS facilities, we have seen that the need for protection to a core workforce is equally critical but for different reasons. In the lean case, the kaizen process drives the need to keep employees from feeling at risk, whereas in the STS setting it is the autonomous decision-making process that necessitates the assurances of employment security. In this case, the assurances support employees as they take on additional operational responsibilities. Placing teams at risk of a layoff is tantamount to placing regular business operations at risk.

In the STS sites, like the lean sites, there were a number of technical and nontechnical jobs handled by part-time and temporary workers. For example, when I/NTek started operations, it was designed to operate with employment security assurances that applied to 80% of the core workforce. The part-time and temporary workers are clearly at risk in these settings.

While we saw above that first-line supervisors were not at as much risk as might be expected in the lean system (due to the need for coordination across teams), there is substantial risk for the first-line supervisor position and even middle manager positions in an STS setting. For example, each turn (or shift) at the startup of I/NTek was organized as a single team, which meant that the average team size was about 32 employees. Subsequently, the team size was reduced to about 18 employees—with no corresponding increase in the number of managers in the facility. A management resource person is available to a team, but most first-line supervisory responsibilities around assigning work, scheduling production, monitoring quality, and even customer relations are handled within the team. Consequently, the first-line supervisor and middle management positions are at great risk in such an STS setting.

In fact, the employment of supervisors and managers in a setting such as I/NTek becomes more precarious over time since knowledge increasingly resides within the teams. As a result, the managers are constrained in their ability to add value in a traditional sense. For example, in the response to the crisis around the rollers, middle managers were less central than senior plant management, union leadership, or the involved workers.

We have seen that employment security assurances for the core workforce are made possible, in part, by the presence of a group of part-time or periphery workers. These people are part-time, temporary, or contract workers who are hired for a variety of reasons. They may be employed as an alternative to expanded overtime hours for the core workforce, or they may work at tasks that other workers cannot or do not do, or they may serve in this role to be evaluated as future potential hires, or they may serve as a buffer against layoffs of the core workforce. These workers are frequently paid less, work on a contract basis, and have little or no employment security. In some organizations, this situation has led to a secondary class of workers who may or may not have opportunities to become part of the regular workforce. In a very real sense, the periphery group exists to increase the security of the core group of regular workers.

At all of our sites that used temporary workers, there was some degree of tension associated with the practice. Attempts were made in a number of the sites to develop paths into the core workforce, both to mitigate the tensions and to take advantage of the information derived from observing the work practices of the temporary workers. At Denso Manufacturing–Michigan, Inc., a system has been developed to allow temporary workers to interview for openings in the core workforce. Hours worked in temporary status accumulate. Workers with the highest number of hours are given the opportunity to interview for up to three core workforce positions. If they do not secure a core position after three interviews, they are encouraged to return to the temporary agency to seek other employment opportunities.

Even when companies had mechanisms that allowed temporary workers to become full-time, core workers felt uncomfortable with the status differential. Also, there were reports of expectations on the part of temporary workers that were not met by actual practice. A key issue to consider centers on the long-term use of these "temporary" workers. Will they continue to bear the risks in the same way when they have long-term associations with the organizations? Also, will their ideas and energy link into kaizen or STS systems when they lack the same assurances as the core workers?

Additional Risks for Organizations and Institutions

The capability of firms to provide employment security assurances varies across groups of employees, each of whom we saw as being at varying degrees of risk. There is also variance across facilities and even firms in the degree of risk. In some plants, the pressures driving test events are less severe than in other facilities owned by the same company. For example, I/NTek is among the newest facilities in either the Inland or the Nippon Steel systems. As such, they are capable of the highest quality and are likely to be assured work even when the hours at other facilities are reduced. Across companies and industries, there are similar differences in the degree to which employment security assurances are easier or harder to provide. For example, product demand in the musical instruments business may be less volatile than in the auto supply business, making it relatively easier to manage the informal practices associated with avoiding layoffs.

The firm- and industry-specific nature of the conditions that support employment security have powerful and complex implications for unions and local managements. To attend to the full range of informal emergent practices associated with assurances of employment security, unions will need to be much more closely connected to firm- and even plant-level decision making and planning. When this relationship develops, unions may be more responsive to the perceived needs of the firm rather than to the priorities of the union at regional or national levels. Union responsibilities such as dispute resolution or bargaining are dealt with more effectively at the lower levels. Furthermore, the union may even come to give priority to the interests of the majority of its members and the interests of the firm, even where a minority of the members is disadvantaged by administrative decisions. This is always a dilemma for a union, but the dilemma may be sharpened where the union builds such close ties with management as it attempts to administer assurances of employment security.

Thus, the variation of circumstances across plants and firms points toward what looks increasingly like an enterprise model of unionism. Most unions that seek employment security assurances do not necessarily see them as being linked to a more decentralized union structure. Yet in settings where there were such assurances, union leaders described frustration in attempting to balance local plant needs with larger international union priorities. Concurrently, it has become very difficult for international unions to service a union local where so much administrative knowledge resides at the plant level.[22] It is of note, however, that the USWA local at I/NTek did get some valuable assistance as a result of the coordinated national efforts of the Steelworkers union on employment security.

Conclusion

Clearly, organizations operating according to lean manufacturing principles or with STS teams must address the issue of employment security. What we have learned, however, is that addressing the issue of employment security is not a one-time event. Rather, there is a substantial degree of learning that must take place within an organization to come to its own understanding of the nature and scope of employment security assurances.

In the Japanese context, there are still many challenges and much learning that is taking place around the issue of employment security. However, there are a number of core dilemmas that are exacerbated in

the U.S. context. For example, tensions associated with a division between core and periphery workers in the workforce are accentuated since
such divisions are not as readily accepted in the U.S. context. Similarly,
the implications of this system for unions are much more controversial
than they are for Japan's enterprise model of unionism.

Our research suggests that employment security has to be understood as an emergent concept and as a reciprocal set of understandings
that take on new meaning with each test event. Furthermore, employment security is constantly evolving through the daily mix of interactions and the resulting body of knowledge created that improves the
performance of the firm. These findings stand in stark contrast to the
current preoccupation of the business press around what can be thought
of as individuals being responsible for their own employment security.
To the extent that work is knowledge driven, more robust employment
security strategies are required. Effectively implementing these strategies enables both individuals and organizations to take on a long-term
perspective, which facilitates the resolution of disputes, the distribution
of rewards, and the creation of new possibilities.

7

Human Resource Management and Knowledge-Driven Work Systems

· ·

Introduction

For most of this century, workers were hired to be a pair of hands to serve a machine. The tasks and goals of what were then referred to as personnel managers were fundamentally different. Under the mass production model, employees were screened for health and ability to withstand the labor of the assembly line. Technical skills were important for a small group of workers involved in craftwork such as die making and pipe fitting. This same logic reached beyond the factories to office and retail settings.

Employee knowledge under the mass production model was valued only where there was clear expertise. Craft-based knowledge, for example, allowed skilled trades workers to bargain as a special case in contract negotiations, while workers with assembly line experience were viewed by most managers as interchangeable parts throughout the industry. High levels of turnover meant that personnel officers were primarily in the business of finding a steady stream of new hands. A worker's time was in effect rented, and an employee's standing with the company was seen as a short-term exchange rather than a long-term relationship.

Knowledge-driven work requires more than a worker's hands. The person must be engaged to think and participate in his or her tasks. Human resource departments must focus on hiring not just technical experts but people at all levels with skills that facilitate team work and participative activities. There is a need for people with flexibility and a willingness to learn new jobs. This focus on what we have termed intangibles stands in sharp contrast with the requirements for workers in mass production. This emphasis requires a radical shift in the attitudes, assumptions, strategies, and goals of the human resource function.

By the mid 1980s, some elements of knowledge-driven production were beginning to emerge in the United States. A particular type of knowledge-driven system, lean production, had by this time developed in Japan over two or three decades.[1] We can never know fully what was in the minds of the leaders of the second-wave firms as they began the process of establishing locations in North America. Still, the evidence in the factories we visited suggests that they chose a piecemeal approach to the adoption of Japanese human resource management practices. For example, they did not choose to include practices such as individual performance appraisal for production and skilled trade workers, seniority-based wages tied to employment security, and selection focused on a careful matching of companies to current college or high school graduates.[2]

Instead, the Japanese firms hired U.S. consultants, human resource professionals, and managers who advised the firms on what they saw as "best practice" in the areas of selection, training, and compensation. As we will see, the second-wave firms that were both opening new facilities and hiring new workforces utilized leading nonunion human resource management practices such as careful psychological screening of large pools of applicants and skill-based pay systems. Although there was not the intentional effort to transfer many Japanese human resource practices, the U.S. practices came to take on new meanings in these settings.

Underlying the variation in human resource management practices is a set of legal constraints and, more important, key assumptions about people. These assumptions center on a long-term employment relationship that values knowledge and investment in people. Organizations that have knowledge-driven work systems must develop appropriate strategies such as redesigned compensation plans, selection practices that focus on multiple competencies, and mechanisms that diffuse information throughout the organization. At a deeper level, these organizations must fashion human resource practices consistent with a very different set of social contracts that are forged between employers and employees.[3]

We will focus on three traditional aspects of human resource management: recruitment and selection, training, and compensation and rewards. These are core parts of the human resources adage "ARM"—attract, retain, and motivate employees.[4]

In all three areas, we observed U.S. practices that contrasted strongly with practices in Japan. These are, therefore, interesting cases where the cross-cultural diffusion is not obvious at the surface. In the final section of this chapter, we turn to the issue of communications, which helps to explain how the practices have come to fit together and evolve in distinctive ways.

Recruitment and Selection

Recruitment and selection processes serve the firm by attracting and hiring qualified employees who possess the required talents and skills. Under the mass production model, recruitment and selection screened for a narrow set of tangible skills and explicit technical know-how seen as functional for the specific job for which the person was being hired.[5] For example, a firm would hire a die maker or a laborer into a defined job classification. The objective was to fit the person into a predefined job.

By contrast, a knowledge-driven work system points to a very different set of recruitment and selection objectives. The screening in this case centers on prospective employees' abilities to be part of a team-based system—to learn multiple jobs and skills and to contribute to on-the-job problem solving. This screening goes beyond a valuing of technical skills and explicit knowledge, pointing also to intangibles such as commitment, flexibility, and enthusiasm as hiring objectives. Here the goal is to match the person's capacity to develop and contribute with the organizational capacity to perform and adapt. Under this system, recruitment and selection represent the ways in which knowledge enters the firm.

There is a coherent logic that underlies recruitment and selection in the case of a knowledge-driven work system, just as there is a logic that underlies the traditional practices. Yet this focus on intangible attributes is a source of great misunderstanding in the U.S. context. Controversy surrounds the recruitment and selection practices of some of the Japanese-affiliated firms operating in the United States. The controversy has almost certainly generated inaccurate stereotyping of many of these firms as relying on young, malleable workers as a competitive advantage.

The controversy is rooted in both anecdotal and more comprehensive studies of the tendency of Japanese firms to locate new operations in smaller, rural, homogeneous communities, as well as the stated preference by some of these firms to operate on a nonunion basis.[6] These tendencies have been folded into public debates on issues of racial and gender discrimination.[7] While the number of factories that we studied is too small to speak directly to overall trends in Japanese investment in North America, a close look at the recruitment and selection practices in these firms reveals a much more complex reality than would be suggested by the public debates.

The issue of where a firm locates was also highly influenced by the competitive offers made by states and regions bidding to attract the jobs that each firm provided. Enticements included tax abatements, initial training subsidies, improved infrastructures, and even building sites. Such issues had more impact than the specific characteristics of the local labor pool.[8]

Location is an issue primarily for the second-wave firms building new facilities and introducing a new work system. In this context, the two first-wave factories that we visited—Hitachi Magnetics and Yamaha Musical Products—used traditional U.S. hiring practices. The primary emphasis was on past work experience, high school diplomas, and technical skills that matched the production system and did not involve the diffusion of Japanese human resources practice.

We observed two very different sets of practices among second-wave firms. First, in the cases of AAI, Denso Manufacturing–Michigan, Inc., Ogihara, and Coil Center, there was extensive recruitment and highly structured selection. Perhaps surprisingly, the initial hiring by these firms did not emphasize past industrial work experience or formal technical skills. Instead, the focus was on intangible factors such as commitment, teamwork orientation, and flexibility. In terms of tangible skills, the focus for production workers was on fine motor skills, lifting capability, attendance records, and educational attainment—not specific tangible work experience such as running a machine. This approach was based on the advice and support of U.S. consultants and human resource professionals hired by the firms. Interestingly, among the four firms, there have been very different implications of these selection practices.

For example, at Ogihara the original selection process involved extensive interviews and tests at a special office set up in Howell, Michigan. Only one in fifty applicants was hired. According to the administration manager, Clyde Nash, workers had to have an ability to learn, and "we don't take someone who doesn't appear to have the work ethic." We were told that the firm wanted "hungry" and ambitious people. Once operations began at Ogihara, the hiring process expanded to include interviews of prospective employees by team facilitators.

At Denso Manufacturing–Michigan, Inc., and Ogihara, these selection practices continued after the first workforces were established. Both organizations have more than doubled in size since they began operations, and both continue to see value in this approach to selection. Many of the operators we met in both organizations had previously worked in professions such as teaching, social work, and sales. This pool of people represents a diverse set of knowledge frameworks. All expressed some surprise at being chosen for their jobs, and they indicated how delighted they were at having the opportunity to earn much more than they had earned in their previous profession. This is a particularly interesting implication of the selection strategy since, as we will see in the section on compensation, the average wages paid in these firms may be high for their communities but are not at the top of the range for first-tier firms in the auto-supply industry (direct suppliers of assembly plants).

By contrast, while the Coil Center still looks for the intangibles of commitment and teamwork, the primary criteria for selection as the workforce expands has been technical skill. The original general manager of the firm, Bill Hollister, explained the shift in terms of a "make or buy" decision. He said that it had proved much more difficult to take people with a positive attitude and make them into technical specialists than to hire the technical specialists. This decision reflects a lack of technical expertise available within the firm and its joint venture partners. At a deeper level the Coil Center has not given the same priority to fostering a knowledge-driven production system as have Denso Manufacturing–Michigan, Inc., and Ogihara.

At AAI, the initial selection process had a different implication. Thousands of people expressed interest in working for AAI when Mazda announced plans to begin hiring. The people ultimately selected came from many walks of life, many without extensive industrial experience. According to Phil Keeling, UAW Local 3000 president, for 80% of the new hires this was their first job.

Unlike the supplier firms, Denso Manufacturing–Michigan, Inc., Ogihara, and the Coil Center, AAI is an assembly plant and began operations organized by the UAW. The result has been quite complicated. When we visited with the local union president, for example, we learned that he did have prior union experience but in the construction trades. Because AAI's workforce did not have deep roots in the UAW, the nature and dynamics of the local union have unfolded in a number of distinct ways.

In the mid 1980s, the initial appointed union leadership worked closely with management at AAI.[9] Then came what is known as the long, hot summer in 1988, when the formal channels were inadequate for handling the grievances on the floor and spontaneous walkouts occurred. This was followed by the election of an entirely new slate of leaders in the local union that has made the production system itself a key issue.

While there are certainly many factors associated with the volatile history at AAI, it is likely that the experience of the newly hired workforce did not meet the expectations of input and involvement they were given during training. The disconnect was even more serious when we consider the expectations of the Japanese managers and engineers. These individuals assumed that everyone would make large sacrifices during production ramp-up because they supposedly shared a common interest in long-term company success. The clash of expectations violated the social contract and destroyed the trust necessary to continue early positive steps in building a high-commitment employment relationship.

As we saw in chapter 6, both the NUMMI and I/NTek workforces transferred workers with industry experience at startup into the newly created firms. There was no initial need for extensive recruitment due to agreements reached with the unions that represented these workers. Formal screening processes existed for workers who were being rehired from the GM Fremont plant and who were working at the Indiana Harbor Mill.

Additional employees have also been hired. The recruitment and selection processes in these cases matched what we describe in the cases of Denso Manufacturing–Michigan, Inc., and Ogihara in focusing on intangibles such as teamwork, commitment, and flexibility. For example, the selection of new workers at NUMMI involved initial screening for drugs, alcohol, and attendance. Then the assessment, following the applicant orientation workshop, focused on flexibility, team skills, leadership, and problem solving. People were being hired into a general production position, not into a specific, narrowly defined job classification.

Thus, we see that the public debates about selection practices at Japanese-affiliated firms fail to capture a very complex reality. The first-wave firms and some of the second-wave firms do not even feature the controversial selection practices. Furthermore, the firms that were utilizing these practices did so on the advice of U.S. consultants based on experience in many domestic nonunion operations. The advice may have been reinforced by a Japanese preference for homogeneity, but this can hardly be characterized as an exclusively Japanese approach to recruitment and selection. Finally, and most important, those settings operating with a knowledge-driven approach have shifted away from the historic focus on hiring people to fit a narrowly defined job and toward matching people with a dynamic and flexible work system. A careful recruitment and selection process alone does not assure success. The elevated expectations associated with such a process can even backfire when reality does not match these expectations. But we observe hiring focused on intangibles as the emerging model to support a knowledge-driven work system.

Training

Under mass production, training served to prepare individuals for specific tasks or as a form of compliance with legal mandates. Even then, training was generally devalued and resisted by managers. By contrast, under a knowledge-driven work system the capability that has entered the firm through selection focused on intangibles is able to reach full potential only through further training and development. Under the former system training is an "add on," while under the latter it is integral and continuous.

Not all of the organizations we visited featured full, knowledge-driven work systems. Not surprisingly, we observed great variation in practice. Key factors accounting for the variation include the timing of the investment, the type of team system, and the link between training and business strategy. The experience with training reinforces and extends dynamics first visible in recruitment and selection.

We observed a level of training in the two first-wave organizations that would be characteristic of many progressive U.S. firms. Both Hitachi Magnetics and Yamaha Musical Products featured employee-involvement and problem-solving training. In both cases, there was also training in compliance with Occupational Safety and Health Act (OSHA) mandates. Though there was some training on technical skills, most production workers received informal, on-the-job training.

The second-wave organizations all featured a much stronger focus on what might be called developmental skills—both individual and organizational development. This is not surprising, given the objective of introducing Japanese work practices in the U.S. context. For example, all but one of these organizations provided opportunities for managers, engineers, supervisors, team leaders, and team members to work and learn in Japan with counterparts in sister or parent factories. The one exception was Coil Center, the smallest organization that we visited, a plant owned by a Japanese trading company that does not have an equivalent Japanese factory.

Among the second-wave firms, however, there were important distinctions between firms where work was organized around what we have termed STS and lean systems. In the case of the two STS organizations, there were high levels of training in group process skills such as decision making and problem solving, all of which were central to the effective functioning of these teams. There was also the full array of standard technical training on issues of safety, quality, and skilled trades. In addition, there was support for furthering education through attendance of college courses. There were high levels of job rotation and cross training in technical skills. Many aspects of the training such as scheduling and planning were all coordinated within the teams.

While Coil Center Corporation began with a similar model and approach to training, the practice became a major source of internal contention when the company expanded and added its second shift. Prior to the expansion, the company was experiencing disruptions in production operations as a result of the cross training within teams. Each worker would spend a month learning a new skill, with all of the rotations occurring during the first week of each month. Consequently, production and quality would both be affected the first week as everyone was struggling to learn new jobs. The workers pushed for each rotation so that they could be certified in yet another skill and move up in the pay-for-knowledge system.

As part of the expansion, the firm reversed its selection process to focus on hiring people who already had technical experience in the steel industry. This decision served to reduce the problems on the first week of each month but introduced a new set of dilemmas as the new highly skilled workers jumped ahead of the more senior employees in the skill certification process. This skill certification system was directly tied to pay, job rotation planning, and promotions. In fact, it was one of these newly hired employees (with extensive prior work experience in the steel industry) who became the team leader on the second shift. He was promoted ahead of employees who had been with the firm much longer, violating their expectations that one of them would lead the new second shift. A social contract was, in effect, broken. Furthermore, this discounted the human capital investment that had been made in these first employees. A knowledge-driven approach to training was undercut when the selection process shifted to focus on hiring people with needed skills rather than developing them.

How do we account for the contrasting experiences at I/NTek and Coil Center Corporation? While both firms vary in terms of size and union status, the most likely explanation lies in the degree to which employee knowledge channeled through autonomous teams was central to the business strategy. In the case of I/NTek, the firm continued to depend on teams (not individuals) to manage their portion of the business operation. Training was the key to maintaining and enhancing this capability. While work continued to be organized around teams, Coil Center Corporation was in the midst of a shift toward increased reliance on a few highly skilled and knowledgeable individuals. This shift from a reliance on the collective knowledge and capability of the team was first visible in the selection process, with direct consequences illustrated by the experience with training.

Among the firms utilizing lean production systems, there were some important parallels concerning the links between training and business strategy. All of the lean firms devoted considerable resources to training. Indeed, two of the firms—NUMMI and Denso Manufacturing–Michigan, Inc.—are world-class benchmark organizations for workplace training. Both firms featured direct integration of training into business strategy. At NUMMI, for example, the importance of training is first reflected in the overall policy on staffing levels. We were told that the firm deliberately hires at a staffing level that allows at least 5% of the workforce to be in training at any given time. This is a fairly remarkable number, which suggests that at any given moment on every shift there will always be about 300 people out of the 6,000-person workforce involved in some form of training.

When NUMMI faced a sharp decline in demand for the Chevrolet Nova, rather than laying anyone off, it created a central pool of workers to be trained as trainers for topics such as group problem solving. In this way, training was the vehicle for making a long-term investment in increased capability of the workforce. At a team level, each work area displays a training matrix listing skills across the top of the chart and the names of the team members down the first column of the matrix (see figure 7.1). Next to each name (and under each skill), there is a pie chart with sections to be filled in as the team member achieves (1) awareness, (2) competence, and (3) ability to teach others in a given skill.

The careful attention to training at Denso Manufacturing–Michigan, Inc., began with new employee orientations that were designed to be held for 2 days in office area conference rooms, followed by a day in meeting rooms off the factory floor, followed by 90 days on the shop floor itself. The goal, we were told, was to ensure that new workers unfamiliar with a factory environment would become increasingly accustomed to the ambient noise and activity. Once an employee was on the floor, the integration of training into team operations was similar to NUMMI, with training matrices posted and clearly visible in each team's hot corner.

At the time of our visits, Denso Manufacturing–Michigan, Inc., was substantially increasing the training of operators in certain technical skills, such as robotics, that were previously reserved for pilot product launches in the Japanese operations. We were told that these skills reflected increasingly close links between the U.S. operations and the U.S. customers around product engineering and redesign. Consequently, it was necessary to invest more heavily in building the shop-floor capability to

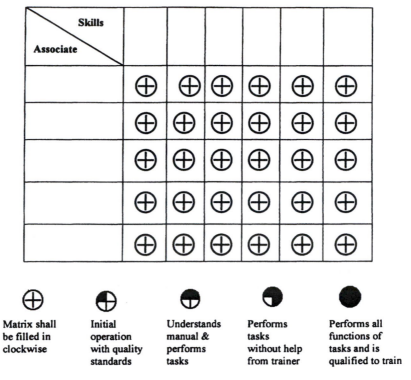

Figure 7.1 Job knowledge matrix. Adapted from a 1998 form used at Denso Manufacturing–Michigan, Inc.

develop and operate next-generation production equipment rather than waiting for the development to take place in Japan.

One simple yet telling sign of the constant flow of training activity at Denso Manufacturing–Michigan, Inc., was the sign-up sheets in the training rooms. Scheduling was done in 5-minute increments, with almost no time in any 24-hour period left unscheduled. When we held focus group interviews or other meetings in these rooms, we learned to be quick and get out of the way at the end of our session because the next group was always at the door and ready to begin its meeting or training session. Now the company schedules in 1-hour increments, but it is still intense. Team leaders at Denso Manufacturing–Michigan, Inc. (who are also first-line supervisors), and team leaders at NUMMI were able to speak with great detail about the individual coaching and development plans they had for each worker in their area. In fact, it became hard to draw a distinction between what was training and what was not. Training was a central part of everyone's job on a continuous basis.

At Ogihara, the structure and role of training was comparable to that at NUMMI and Denso Manufacturing–Michigan, Inc., though perhaps not as extensive in intensity. In all three organizations, leading employees are sent back to Japan to be taught tangible and intangible skills. In the case of Ogihara the learning of tangible skills is limited by the fact that the company has no stamping operations in Japan. Interestingly, the expertise built in the U.S. location is diffusing globally. Workers from Ogihara's plant in Howell were sent to assist Chrysler in setting up a stamping plant in Mexico for the new Neon automobile. Clearly, training in the context of a knowledge-driven work system takes on a strategic role unlike anything in a traditional work system.

A more complicated puzzle arises in the case of AAI, however. Like the other three firms featuring lean manufacturing systems, AAI did have job rotation, posted training matrices, and extensive levels of technical and developmental training. Yet our conversations with workers and managers at AAI did not reveal the same degree to which training was seen as essential to continuous improvement in daily operations. Training in safety and technical skills was clearly valued and judged important, but workers spoke only of completing skills rotations for progression through a pay system, not of ways in which the cross training contributed to an increased ability to solve problems and enable improvements.[10] At a tangible level, the amount of training was exceptionally high in all four lean organizations. It was, however, the intangibles having to do with the links between training, organizational strategy, and individual development that accounted for a wide divergence between viewing training as an add-on activity and seeing it as an integrated part of daily operations.

Compensation and Reward Systems

Compensation and reward systems are generally assumed to attract, retain, and motivate employees—though there is great debate over the degree to which this is actually the case. Pay can be seen as a cost to the organization or as an investment. Similarly, pay can be seen as a key driver of desired behaviors or as a barrier to a focus on intrinsic motivation. What we saw in the field directly speaks to these debates. The Japanese-affiliated organizations we studied did not rely on pay to attract new workers or to drive high levels of commitment.

In the first-wave firms, there were few links between pay and commitment. The work system was premised primarily on worker compliance. Both Yamaha Musical Products and Hitachi Magnetics were regarded as providing well-paying jobs in their respective communities, but there was no intangible link between the level of pay and any expectation of commitment on the parts of management and labor.

There were compensation issues in the first-wave firms, but they were issues not unlike the challenges faced by many domestic firms. For example, the union and management at Hitachi Magnetics had negotiated a prior contract with a two-tier wage system. At the time of our visits, the lower-tier employees expressed significant dissatisfaction. Internal disruption in the union was anticipated as this group of people was approaching 50% of the union membership.

The more interesting cases, of course, are in the second-wave firms where high levels of worker involvement and commitment were seen as essential to continuous improvement. Among the second-wave firms, compensation did vary by union status. The unionized sites (NUMMI, AAI, and I/NTek) had maintained pay levels in their contracts that were only slightly below the levels in the national agreements (at General Motors, Ford, and Inland Steel respectively).

Both NUMMI and I/NTek featured pay-for-knowledge systems with increased pay levels based on skills learned. The average worker in these plants enjoyed levels of pay and benefits roughly comparable to workers in their sister U.S. locations. At NUMMI, the average annual pay was in the $45,000 to $65,000 range in the early 1990s. There was relatively little discussion of pay in our meetings with workers or managers in these two settings. The only issue that did surface was at I/NTek, where the pay-for-knowledge system was not fully operational and progression was based on time in a job rather than on any demonstration of competence with certification by others. At NUMMI, there was a full system of certification by team leaders and others in place.

In contrast with workers at NUMMI and I/NTek, people at other organizations with pay-for-knowledge systems often appear preoccupied with progression through the pay system. Based on our observations, we anticipate the difference reflects the attempt to use pay to drive improvements as compared to a knowledge-based pay system where improvement is driven primarily by the structure of daily work operations. The dilemma for the U.S. employers may be how to balance the fairness issues of evaluation, skill assessment, and motivation with the competency demands of the organization. Clearly, pay should not be inconsistent with the work system, but pay alone can't drive the improvement activities.

The reduced salience of pay was even more evident in the nonunion operations we visited. Ogihara, Denso Manufacturing–Michigan, Inc., and Coil Center Corporation all had made choices *not* to be pay leaders in their areas. Workers at Ogihara, for example, told us that it was perfectly acceptable for them to receive lower pay than other auto suppliers were so that they could be more competitive. The top wage at Ogihara in the mid 1990s was $16.30 per hour. To some degree, the observations of the workers at Ogihara reflect those from the individuals who had been teachers, social workers, or sales representatives. These were all professionals who received pay increases when they shifted to industrial work. However, workers who had been at Ogihara for a long time accepted these pay practices. This was well after these workers would have compared their pay to that of their previous professions. We even heard this from former unionized workers. Workers in these locations told us that pay levels of even $4 or $5 per hour less than traditional auto jobs were an acceptable trade-off given the higher levels of employment security and the fact that they liked what they were doing at work. As the administration manager at Ogihara, Clyde Nash, put it:

> The company has a low to moderate salary structure but a safe job for
> its employees. Employees don't have the fear of losing their jobs. They
> are reasonably secure about their jobs. What is happening in GM places
> is that the union can't provide them job security.

A team leader at Ogihara echoed similar sentiments when he stated, "I'd rather have less money and work longer than make more money and not know if I can afford the house for my wife and kids." In discussing the competitive need for lower wages, another team leader stated, "You've got to beat their price and be good these days."

All three of the nonunion firms had just one job classification for production workers. At I/NTek, there were five classifications, and NUMMI had one classification for production and two for skilled trades. By contrast, Yamaha Musical Products had 10 separate pay grades and Hitachi Magnetics had 63 job classifications (reduced from 93 in the 1991 negotiations).

Within the nonunion firms with single classifications, pay increases were tied to learning more skills. Both Denso Manufacturing–Michigan, Inc., and Coil Center, for example, have three levels of skill for a production worker. Associates at Denso Manufacturing–Michigan, Inc., progress from qualified to proficient to advanced by learning additional skills in their work areas, with pay increases for each promotion within the associate classification. At Coil Center, people are promoted from team level 1 to 2 to 3 based on the number of tasks learned out of a possible 26. Ogihara did not have the three levels but instead provided fixed dollar increases for each new job learned.

One interesting feature of the reward system at Coil Center is that performance appraisals were conducted on six factors: attendance, safety, hygiene, business, operations, and equipment. A small portion of pay (approximately 5%) was at risk based on these performance appraisals. On the surface it would seem that this represents an adoption of the

Japanese practice of conducting performance appraisals for industrial workers with a portion of pay at risk. In fact, this practice was introduced by the U.S. manager, and we were told it had no link to the Japanese owners.

Interestingly, the same reduced emphasis on compensation in most of the second-wave sites was also reflected in the pay practices for managers. At Denso Manufacturing–Michigan, Inc., and Ogihara, for example, we were told that managerial pay was well below industry norms as part of a strategy of minimizing pay differentials between hourly and production workers. In both cases, however, the firms reported problems with managerial turnover because in part managers with experience in these leading Japanese firms are seen as bringing highly valued knowledge to U.S. workplaces. In fact, Ogihara Vice President Henry Soneoka reports that they are increasingly setting management pay based on market benchmarking.

Further complicating the picture on management pay was the fact that the Japanese managers and engineers located in these organizations were still receiving pay and benefits in accordance to their role and status in Japan. In most cases, these Japanese employees were compensated on a different scale that was devised to reflect their concerns such as maintaining a family in Japan or moving them to this country. Pay differential might depend on a number of factors such as which division of an organization was paying the employee's salary or the relationship to promotional opportunities in the firm in Japan.[11] All these elements may lead to the frequent perception of pay inequity that arises between Japanese and U.S. managers.

Thus, we conclude that a knowledge-driven work system does not depend on pay to drive continuous improvement, but it does depend on pay not being a barrier. In the case of production workers, both the union and nonunion second-wave settings had successfully minimized the degree to which pay was a salient issue in daily operations—through tangible assurances regarding employment security and intangible aspects of a workplace culture characterized by respect and appreciation of worker knowledge. On the other hand, we observed some complicated and still unresolved issues concerning compensation for managers and professionals.

Communication

If this were only a chapter on human resources in traditional systems, we would not even have a section on communications or, if there were one, it would primarily focus on unidirectional communication—from the bottom up, from the top down, or in from 360 degrees. Our focus is on the multidirectional patterns of communication that are at the heart of human resource practices in a knowledge-driven work system.[12] In communication practices, as in so many other areas, we see that actions have different meanings. For example, talking among workers in a mass production setting is frequently regarded as time when people are not working. In a knowledge-driven system talking among workers must occur as a critical element of problem solving, improvement efforts, and knowledge creation. In other words the ability to interact with other workers and the work organization system is integral to the success of the production process. Thus, vital tangible and intangible workplace factors depend on communication in a variety of forms.

A primary task in creating effective communication in a knowledge-driven workplace is the job of ensuring the transformation of individual and collective tacit knowledge into explicit knowledge that may be used by the firm.[13] When workers meet to discuss workplace problems, they bring their individual tacit knowledge and experiences to the discussion. As they talk they create virtual knowledge, which can lead to explicit knowledge aimed at a specific problem or issue. Human-resource management functions are closely interrelated to the entire system of work organization and production. Selection and hiring practices in our second-wave sites in particular focus on nurturing a workforce with a great degree of potential for change and high levels of interpersonal skills.

In table 7.1, we provide a visual overview of the multiple channels of communication we observed in our sites. On one hand this table represents the visual aspects of some of the workplaces we visited. How are this table and the communication it represents connected to the human-resource management activities of a competitive firm?

As table 7.1 illustrates, all of the organizations featured multiple mechanisms for communication. There is a far more dense set of mechanisms for on-line teams (either lean teams or STS teams), reflecting the increased formal communication at that level. However, one of the important lessons to be derived from table 7.1 concerns what cannot be represented in the table. Even where there are similar mechanisms for communication in two sites, the content and quality of the communication process can vary considerably. These are intangible aspects of the communication.

In a knowledge-driven work system, communication serves two key roles. First, it is the process by which variation (in the form of new ideas) is surfaced. Second, it is also the mechanism by which the new ideas are standardized into regular operations. In this respect, investment in communication is not just a nice thing to do; it is an essential requirement of the system.

Table 7.1 Multiple Mechanisms for Communication

Channels/Activities	Hitachi	Yamaha	Coil Center Corporation	I/N Tek/Kote	AAI	NUMMI	Denso Manufacturing, Inc.	Ogihara
Meetings								
Daily "shift start" team meetings			Yes	Yes		Yes	Yes	Yes
Formal weekly team meetings			Yes	Yes	Yes	Yes	Yes	Yes
Monthly team/departmental meetings	Yes	Yes	Yes	Yes	Yes	Yes	Yes	Yes
Formal Groups								
Issue-specific task forces (off-line teams)	Yes	Yes	Yes	Yes	Yes	Yes	Yes	Yes
QC/EI/QWL problem-solving groups	Yes	Yes	Yes	Yes	Yes	Yes	Yes	Yes
Standing committees (e.g. safety)	Yes	Yes	Yes	Yes	Yes	Yes	Yes	Yes
General Communication								
Bulletin boards	Yes	Yes	Yes	Yes	Yes	Yes	Yes	Yes
TV monitors with news updates					Yes		Yes	
Newsletter		Yes	Yes	Yes	Yes	Yes	Yes	Yes
Posted slogans	Yes			Yes	Yes	Yes	Yes	Yes
Production Specific								
Andon boards					Yes	Yes	Yes	Yes
Posted plant and team performance measurable			Yes	Yes	Yes	Yes	Yes	Yes
Shift-to-shift logs	Yes	NA	Yes			Yes	Yes	
Other								
Suggestion program	Yes		Yes	Yes	Yes	Yes	Yes	Yes
Open office areas				Yes	Yes	Yes	Yes	Yes

Traditionally, human resource managers communicated through static information-dissemination mediums, channels that are clearly demarcated from the bureaucratic organizational structure. Bulletin boards and memos, reports and manuals, as well as routine staff meetings are used to deliver company policies and information from top management. In the knowledge-driven system, these channels are flexible, evolving, and closely connected to the shop floor. Interestingly, all of the same media are used, but they serve to share information for the purpose of knowledge creation.

Traditional settings have off-line communication that can occur at a distance from the production line. This communication is not immediate or embedded in the production process and business strategy. This differs from the on-line communication that occurs in knowledge-driven systems as the workers interact in their teams or as a problem occurs on the line. For example, we observed a scene at a Toyota plant that illustrates this issue. An assembly line worker and an engineer were discussing a problem with the worker's tool cart. The tool cart was designed to move along the line with the worker and some problem had arisen. To fix the problem, the engineer had come out to the line to see the situation firsthand. What was even more unusual was the fact that the conversation was occurring on the moving assembly line. The engineer was kneeling on the moving line and observing the problem as it occurred. This was literally on-line problem solving.

This interchange would be very different in a traditional site. Typically, the worker would tell his supervisor about the problem. The supervisor would contact the engineering department. Information is indirectly shared and the problem may be solved much later when the line is shut down. If the worker is not included in the problem solving, valuable tacit knowledge never enters the problem-solving process and there is less opportunity to create direct experiential knowledge for use in other areas of the facility.

Physical settings also symbolize one way in which communication takes place. For example, open office areas at Denso Manufacturing–Michigan, Inc., Ogihara, and NUMMI visually demonstrate to all workers, as well as visitors, the importance of fast, direct, unencumbered information flow. The layout requires communication and cooperation since the physical setting can no longer hide unproductive activities. Hot corners and designated meeting areas are physical signals of the importance of human interaction, interteam competitiveness, and production.

It is a fascinating observation that in some of the companies we visited there are inviting and well-outfitted cafeterias. These were deliberately designed places for workers to eat, congregate, and talk with one another. The food was varied and delicious. American, Japanese, Chinese, Italian, and Mexican cuisine were frequently available. We were surprised to find members of the surrounding community invited in to the cafeteria at Ogihara. The Japanese rock garden at the center of AAI's cafeteria was restful and unexpected. At NUMMI, we observed diverse groups of workers eating and talking together. The diversity went beyond gender, status, and ethnicity to handicapped individuals who were receiving on-the-job training.

Meetings are also integral parts of a work organization. We observed meetings taking place at every level of the operation, formally and informally, on-site and off-site, and scheduled in varying degrees of regularity. At some companies, teams met on a daily or weekly basis, while at other firms teams met on a monthly basis. However, at each of the places we visited plantwide meetings were held. At meetings in traditional settings communication is basically one way. In knowledge-driven settings, communication occurs across groups and levels of organization. Nonaka and Takeuchi name this "middle-up-down" communication.[14] The system cannot function without interactions, which is the key to generating options and enabling improvement.

Table 7.1 shows fewer regularly scheduled opportunities for people to communicate in traditional settings. For example, instead of daily meetings, there were weekly or monthly meetings. Some types of specialized communication, such as task forces, problem-solving groups, and newsletters, occur across all of the firms. In knowledge-driven settings, there are more opportunities for shop-floor workers to instigate communication. People's insights and their ability to contribute to the organization are valued and recognized.

The phrase "knowledge is power" has widely varying meanings in the different production systems we describe. In mass production knowledge is used for control by all the participants. Management controls knowledge about production targets, actual profit margins, product design, personnel decisions (hiring and law), and capital investment. The union traditionally has a more complete knowledge of the contract, frames the issues that are surfaced during problem solving, has the potential to control the flow of work, and maintains a hold on job security through job classifications and seniority systems. Workers control their individual performances and the amount of individual knowledge they apply to the tasks.

In knowledge-driven production systems, knowledge is power that enables. The most crucial difference is the degree to which knowledge and information are shared among all the stakeholders in the workplace. Today, firms are involved in interdependent networks within which information must flow from a source inward and outward to suppliers, customers, and organizational levels. Increasingly, management understands that full disclosure and open books lead to greater employee involvement and competitiveness. Many unions see that their interests and management's are more closely intertwined than ever. Each party understands that power lies in driving work forward rather than withholding it. Workers find greater dignity, recognition in their daily work, and the potential to have a real impact on their work settings.

In their book *The Knowledge-Creating Organization*, Nonaka and Takeuchi discuss the necessity of creating redundancy of information and knowledge among the workforce. In this theory workers across the organization must possess more knowledge than they need to complete their daily tasks. We believe this relates closely to our concept of a broad or narrow gap in what we have come to term "the simultaneous meaning of events." That is, when an event occurs, it is seen from multiple perspectives, and different meanings are simultaneously generated. Where there is a narrow gap, the ability to construct knowledge is strong. Where there is a large gap in meanings that are attributed to the event, then dialogue is needed to narrow the gap before knowledge generation can begin. Team leaders or group leaders who carry information across groups or hierarchical levels in the organization help to prevent gaps in simultaneous meaning. In this respect, they play a pivotal role in the communication process.

Within an organization, there are many functions that are integral to communication. For example, the andon mechanism normally associated with a lean production system symbolizes a set of assumptions about the value of knowledge creation. When a worker needs to alert others to a problem, he or she pulls the andon cord to signal for help and may stop the production line. The problem is addressed by workers and team leaders who bring their tacit knowledge and shared experience to the place where the problem has been identified. This process allows for robust communications in sharing knowledge between workers and across levels of the organization so it can be used in the future.

This stands in stark contrast with the mass production system. In a mass production system, workers could be given a week off without pay as punishment if they stop the assembly process. When a worker discovers a defect at a station the item is marked with a repair ticket and shipped to an off-line repair area at the end of the process. There is often no communication feedback between the repair area and the spot where the defect has occurred. While data are created about the number and kinds of repairs completed at the end of the process, knowledge that can prevent problems from recurring is not created.[15] In knowledge-driven production, workers' actions are encouraged by systems elements such as training, long-term rewards, peer recognition, effective company performance, and employment security.

Some mass producers have attempted to introduce tangible elements of lean production such as the andon system. However, unless such intangible elements of communication as trust and respect for the ideas of workers are present, the andon system will not improve quality or productivity. Communication is a foundation for knowledge creation and is vital for operating an integrated production system that does not rely on buffers or end-of-the-line repair.

In effect, in knowledge-driven production systems the intangibles shape the tangible elements of the production system. Throughout this book, we have talked about the importance of virtual knowledge. Communication is the essence of knowledge creation: tacit, virtual, and explicit. In knowledge-driven systems, therefore, all human resource functions such as selection and hiring, training, communication, compensation, and reward systems assume an increased significance because of the added importance of people in the organization.

Conclusion

Human resource practices open a door through which the tacit knowledge of workers enters, develops, and interacts with the firm. This points to the essential need for well-thought-out planned selection, hiring, and training practices. The workforce of the future will need to have high levels of interpersonal skills and the ability to anticipate and respond to a constantly changing set of shop-floor conditions. The people who work in the most successful firms today are flexible and prepared to meet new and unexpected competitive conditions.

Knowledge-driven firms hire for the long term—not renting the worker's time but building a sustained interdependent relationship. This leads to a series of assumptions about the relationship and the mutual responsibility that fuels the social contract. Firms invest in the people they hire and train. The largest return on this investment can be recovered only over a long-term relationship. Workers develop new relationships with their employers, and these relationships are strengthened over time. In unionized settings this adaptation and shift in bargaining issues reflects the movement toward more complementary relationships.[16]

Effective knowledge creation is a continuous revitalization of the details of the workplace and the work relationships. If worker knowledge is the vital component of today's competitive organization, the work of human resource professionals will also mean emphasizing new knowledge and continuous learning. Human resource professionals must know the details of the organization's production system in order to appreciate how traditional personnel practices must change to support knowledge-driven work settings. The human resource function must become more long term and strategic, removing barriers to the flow of tacit and explicit knowledge necessary to enable everyone to maximize their contribution. In effect, the human resource people move from being a screen or filter to being a nexus for learning, excitement, and creativity.

8

Labor Relations
· ·

Introduction

After observing examples of the global diffusion of knowledge-driven work systems, we find ourselves unable to describe these factories' labor relations in the traditional language of the field. The words "adversarial" and "enterprise" are commonly used in discussions about U.S. and Japanese labor relations, respectively. In fact, our experience leads us to conclude that these words are not only inadequate but misleading.

Labor relations in the United States are typically referred to as adversarial. United States labor law was written in response to bitter strikes in the 1930s and is premised on the assumption that government must regulate an almost inevitable conflict between unions and employers.[1] Japan is typically referred to as having an enterprise-oriented industrial relations system. In this context, each business is associated with a separate union. Career paths for managers will sometimes involve time spent in union leadership, signaling a much more interdependent relationship between employer and union.

Ironically, the foundations of labor law in Japan are based on the National Labor Relations Act in the United States. Thus, within much the same "adversarial" legal structure a very different system has evolved in Japan. Labor relations, especially in the U.S.–Japanese context, has always been seen to consist of two models—adversarial and enterprise. This distinction is, however, too superficial to help make sense of the multifaceted, emerging patterns we observed.

In this chapter, we will highlight three interrelated themes or distinctions that are more helpful in making sense of what we observed. These are as follows:

1. the knowledge-driven nature of labor relations and the variation that arises in response to system constraints;
2. the symmetrical and complementary patterns of labor and management relationships;
3. the tangible and intangible components that shape labor relations.

To understand what has led us to these themes, first note that U.S. labor management relations have always been in a continuous process of change. The most recent major shift has been the rise in the 1970s and early 1980s of a nonunion human resource management model that began to set the agenda in unionized workplaces.[2] Coincident with the second wave of Japanese investment in the early to mid 1980s, a trans-formation of perhaps greater magnitude has begun.[3] In these second-wave worksites, both sides brought into their new labor–management relationships assumptions about Japanese and U.S. labor relations. Con-cepts such as enterprise unionism, lifetime employment, and the perceived Japanese "exploitation" of workers were the hot topics of debate in the popular press. The prevailing view at the time was that Japanese work practices could not succeed with an American workforce. Second-wave investors also brought with them their fears about whether U.S. unions could step out of their adversarial traditions and whether U.S. workers could match the level of performance of the Japanese workforce.

A close look at the experiences in Japanese-affiliated facilities oper-ating in North America reveals that many of the initial fears were un-founded. Other consequences, however, reach far beyond the debates of the late 1980s. For example, despite fears about the productivity of the U.S. workforce, workers in U.S. operations have been able to ap-proach and sometimes exceed the performance of their Japanese coun-terparts.[4] Far more interesting, however, is the unfolding co-evolution of Japanese and American industrial relations practices taking place.

In this chapter, we will first examine the three work systems—mass, STS, and lean—in terms of the knowledge-driven nature of labor rela-tions. This leads to a contemporary reanalysis of these three systems. We highlight the shift from mass production to two very different knowl-edge-driven systems. As the context of labor relations changes, the be-liefs of the participants in each system also change. Changing beliefs and assumptions about knowledge are at the core of our story.

A Shift to Knowledge-Driven Production

Look beyond the surface institutions of collective bargaining, contract administration, and daily supervision. At its core, the function of labor relations centers on the struggle to place value on the knowledge of employees. It is not typical to define labor relations in terms of knowledge, but doing so helps to point out unexpected ways that the two are intertwined. The internal and external job markets do place a value on many forms of explicit knowledge. For example, college degrees, mastery of skilled trades, and other forms of explicit knowledge do have values placed on them through pay differentials, incentive payments, and other such arrangements. This insight has emerged from our research and has implications that reach far beyond the eight factories we studied. Under craft production, skilled worker knowledge was central to daily operations. The emergence of scientific management and mass production served to discount and stifle that knowledge. Over time, this led to a deeply ingrained managerial belief that workers had little knowledge. Or, if workers did have knowledge, they could not be trusted to use it constructively.

Once workers' knowledge was no longer driving daily operations, a system of rules emerged to guide behavior. In this context, union and management energies focused on increasing the codification and specification of rules. These rules were always at least one step removed from daily workplace realities, so an informal set of understandings also emerged. Unions would either force fit problems into the rules or create new rules to solve past problems.[5] Managers, in taking an adversarial stance toward either union response, would escalate the level of dispute by further separating it from the original problems.

As the rules and the rule-making process became institutionalized, both unions and employers found it increasingly difficult to hear or fully appreciate the knowledge that resided at the point of production or service delivery. The roles enacted by employees, employers, and union officials evolved into stylized patterns of behavior. Occasionally, mediators and arbitrators would bring the parties back to the original problem, but they would as often serve to reinforce and ossify the system of rules.

Sociotechnical Systems

The emergence of the sociotechnical systems model had two distinct yet interrelated implications for labor relations. Managers in knowledge-driven STS firms placed many traditional labor relations responsibilities on work groups, group leaders, and first-line supervisors. In their efforts to foster high levels of commitment, managers regarded adversarial relations as inconsistent. Hence, substantial resources were devoted in North America to build plants in rural areas where workers were less likely to be unionized.[6] Unions were seen as inconsistent with this model. For example, the nonunion plants run by Proctor and Gamble and Cummins Engine (Jamestown, New York) are among many that have been documented in the literature.[7] Thus, one consequence of the STS model was to fuel the rise of a high commitment nonunion model of what became termed "human resource management."[8]

Interestingly, the roots of this STS model in England and Scandinavia were almost all in unionized settings. A number of high-profile union plants also operated in North America with the STS model, including the Shell Sarnia plant, the GM Saturn operations, and the I/NTek steel works. In these cases, a model of labor relations emerged that involved deep labor-management partnerships and dramatic reductions in the use of contractual rules to guide behavior. The 27-page initial Saturn agreement, signed in 1985, was a contrast to the many volumes and the hundreds of pages in the traditional UAW–GM contract. This sort of brief statement of principles was possible because of the higher value placed on the knowledge of workers.

Many unions are concerned that the STS approach will be used as a vehicle for undercutting or escaping unions. In fact, the rural STS "greenfield" plants have tended to remain nonunion. Still, in locations where the workforce is represented by a union, the leaders and members place great value on the way this system reinforces worker autonomy and the way it addresses links between workers and technology. The partnerships are facilitated by the fact that the STS model still relies on buffers. Thus, time can be set aside for team meetings and problem-solving activity by building extra inventory or allowing inputs to stockpile. Also, the knowledge of employees is channeled primarily toward improving safety and work design and less toward the more controversial issues of increasing efficiency or reducing waste. The large number of union officials in many of these settings serves as yet another buffer that facilitates worker and team autonomy.

Lean Production

The rise of the lean production model represents a unique new development in the context of this labor relations history. It is a knowledge-driven system like STS, but it is a system where the knowledge of employees is more directly linked to production. As in STS operations, workers in lean systems have a greater degree of control over the detail of daily operations. In contrast with an STS system, however, the lack of buffers dramatically shifts power relations. Management is vulnerable to even mildly discontent, while workers are expected to drive continuous improvement in production operations or service delivery. Through mechanisms like kaizen, workers can add to the knowledge base of the organization. Of equal importance is the recognition and appreciation of this knowledge creation by the supervisors and managers in the firm.

Managers' roles have shifted from the Tayloristic model—a manager is a source of information that flows down to the workforce—to a more facilitative model. In lean production, managers, group leaders, and team leaders are all part of a network that interacts with the rest of the organization to ensure the optimum use of all types of resources. For example, in a mass production workplace workers who reported an oil leak might be forced to file a health and safety grievance to get it fixed. However, the oil leak in a lean production setting is likely to be fixed expeditiously by multiskilled workers who work in the area. Lean production workers may be more likely to solve noncontractual issues using an established problem-solving procedure rather than file a grievance. Firms have begun to learn that effectiveness rests in the workforce and is enhanced by helping workers resolve obstacles to the flow of work.

At NUMMI, we were told by Bill Childs, executive vice president for human resources, that "if the union says there is a problem, there is a problem." This reflects assumptions and attitudes that would be almost unbelievable for workers in most unionized mass production settings.[9] Workers' knowledge is implicitly respected, sought, and trusted because it is integral to the system. This is an underlying belief that challenges both union and management actions throughout the system.

While tensions and strong feelings do not disappear in this type of environment, many problems that might have been subjected to a costly and time-consuming grievance process can be resolved more quickly. An important additional aspect of this type of system is that problems are resolved much closer to the source of the concern rather than in an institutionalized format with a prescribed set of potential resolutions. For example, when a potential grievance arises at NUMMI, the UAW committeeperson and the management labor relations representative will jointly respond by going out onto the floor, interviewing the people involved, following a problem-solving methodology, and identifying a mutually acceptable solution. Not all problems are resolved so neatly, but many are. In these cases, the rules are shaped to solve problems and then may be changed by mutual agreement as a need arises.

Dynamics across Systems

In contrast to mass production, a knowledge-driven production system, lean or STS, will treat worker complaints or concerns as problems to be solved rather than as grievances to be contested. In mass production, achieving business goals is central to sustaining the system. Worker priorities can be ignored and the system will still function. Among knowledge-driven systems, however, there are important differences in the way in which representatives surface and address worker complaints and concerns.

In an STS workplace, ignoring the social elements will destroy the work system. This is the exact reverse of the mass production system. Union officials and managers, in this context, both face strong institutional constraints in addressing issues around reduction of waste-cutting costs and increasing efficiency. Process consultants end up playing a critical role in these settings by serving as a buffer between labor and management. Remember that the STS context has as its goal optimizing the match between people and technology. With this as the goal, a strong partnership between union and management is relatively easy to forge. The challenge for sociotechnical systems is to develop effective ways to reduce costs while maintaining effective conflict resolution mechanisms without destroying labor-management relations.

In contrast, a lean production system directly links people with business goals and objectives. Issues of increasing efficiency and reducing waste are expected to be at the core of the agenda. These are still very challenging issues for union leaders and managers, but their energies are focused on maintaining a balance between business goals and the interests of the workforce. Labor and management must come to share a strong belief that both objectives are essential to the firm's success. Neither business goals nor people's interests can be ignored.

The differences in labor relations between the lean system and the sociotechnical system reflect the basic goals of the two systems. Both place greater value on treating worker concerns as legitimate problems to be solved. They vary in the types of problems that are given the greatest priority. Also, each has a different potential blind side. An STS operation overlooks highly contentious issues such as reducing waste and increasing efficiency. The blind side of a lean system is the very real potential for increasing business efficiency at the expense of people issues such as health and safety.[10]

Broader Implications

If, as we believe, labor relations is the struggle to place value on the tacit knowledge of workers, then the combined experience in STS and lean settings forces a fundamental reexamination of what we mean by labor relations. Legitimizing the importance and value of worker knowledge is a complex thought for managers, union leaders, and even the workers themselves. It alters the framework and starting point for any discussions in collective bargaining or on the shop floor. Table 8.1 contrasts three accepted terms of collective bargaining from the viewpoints of the traditional and knowledge-driven systems.

In a new era in which the relationships are structured in a more interdependent way, the area of shared interest is much larger. Unions and managements must now discuss a broader range of topics that expand the concepts of wages, hours, and conditions of work to include areas long considered management's sole domains. There is greater recognition of the common interests associated with strategic managerial decisions regarding outsourcing, new technology, quality, and training. As

Table 8.1   The Impact of Work Organization Systems on Collective Bargaining Issues

Collective bargaining issues	Mass	Knowledge-driven
Employment security	An elaborate set of rules developed to govern fairness in layoffs. Job security protected by seniority. Rules reflect assumptions that cutting labor costs is an inevitable, cyclical activity.	Job security protected through explicit language. An implicit social contract recognizes the value of worker experience and skills. Recognition that workers and managers share common interests in the success of the firm during periods of economic growth as well as downturns.
Grievance procedure	An integral part of collective bargaining. Contract enforcement rather than a problem-solving process. Used also to call attention to problems that do not naturally fall into the domain of collective bargaining.	Problem-solving processes allow workers to surface noncontractual issues. The grievance procedure is used to resolve contractual issues that cannot be resolved in another way.
Health and safety concerns*	Health and safety issues enforceable through contractual process and legal and adjudicating agencies. Since management must respond, health and safety provisions frequently function as a catchall within which many other types of problems can be addressed.	Health and safety issues still controlled by legal structures; however, the organizational response focuses on prevention. Kaizen processes help prevent or address problems early. Moreover, worker knowledge is valued and must be protected.

*Frequently, use of health and safety provisions in traditional systems is seen as an expedited way to focus organizational resources on the problem. So an issue may be resolved in a "short time." Contrast this to the response in knowledge-driven systems, which may be immediate.

we saw at I/NTek (see chapter 6), union involvement in making decisions concerning the new rollers' quality problems was not a coincidence.[11] The union ended up playing a central role in what was the ultimate organizational response to the crisis. To discuss these wider areas of interest, the parties must have larger sets of shared knowledge and be willing to exchange much more detailed information than ever before. This information cannot just be shared at the bargaining table or during negotiations, but it must be routinely available.

Both parties must also take on added mutual responsibilities. The larger relationship changes, in part, through this willingness to share and properly use heretofore protected information. At a more personal level, both labor and management leaders must develop new appreciation for the pressures that individuals from each side face from their constituencies. This may mean, for example, that it will no longer be possible to use the other side as a convenient scapegoat.

At another level of the relationship, the parties must ensure that the people they represent are also informed and have equal access to information to effectively participate in the process. The tacit knowledge of each worker becomes the base for mechanisms (such as kaizen and formalized problem solving) that improve the operations of an organization. With this resource at risk, leaders must take great care to continually develop the knowledge base and skills of each member of the workforce. Given the importance of this process to the success of the firm, both labor and management leaders must address these needs at the bargaining table.

Challenging Traditional Measures

As we began our study, there seemed to be measures or characteristics that helped us to understand the types of events that could be observed in a workplace. Table 8.2 contains four of these standard characteristics: union status, work organization system, ownership, and new workforce. None of these elements seems to predict or describe the variation in labor-management relations that we observed.

We visited sites that were greenfield as well as brownfield, lean as well as traditional and STS production systems. Some were organized by unions and some were not. Some were wholly owned by Japanese firms while others were joint U.S.–Japanese ventures. At all of our sites, we found relationships that do not fit neatly into any of these categories.

These structural and tangible factors are typically used to explain variation in labor–management relations. For example, the distinction between unionized and nonunion operations was central to the analysis in *The Transformation of American Industrial Relations*.[12] Many observ-

Table 8.2 Organizations Classified by Traditional Labor
Relations Measures

Sites in order of investment	Union status	Work organization system	Ownership structure	Newly hired workforce
Hitachi	Unionized	Traditional	Wholly owned subsidiary	No Existing General Electric workforce
Yamaha	Unionized	Traditional	Wholly owned subsidiary	Yes/No Existing Baker Piano Co. workforce & new workforce
NUMMI	Unionized	Lean	Joint venture	No Existing GM workforce
Mazda/AAI	Unionized	Lean	Joint venture	Yes New workforce
Denso	Nonunion	Lean	Wholly owned subsidiary	Yes New workforce
Ogihara	Nonunion	Lean	Wholly owned subsidiary	Yes New workforce
Coil Center	Nonunion	STS	Joint venture	Yes New workforce
I/NTek	Unionized	STS	Joint venture	Yes/No Transfers* & new hires

*Transfers from Inland Steel

ers of Japanese-affiliated operations have placed great emphasis on issues of ownership and the use of greenfield sites with new workforces.
In the organizations we studied, we discovered that the customary ways
of describing labor relations did not help us understand what we were
seeing.

Symmetrical and Complementary

At NUMMI, the distinction between adversarial labor relations in the
United States and enterprise labor relations in Japan was thrown into
sharp relief. Certainly, the union and employer had a less "adversarial"
relationship than many other UAW–GM locations. Similarly, the management of employment security and other location-specific matters was
creating many dilemmas for the union that echoed the concept of enterprise unionism. But these terms failed to capture or reflect a much
more complex and subtle set of labor relations challenges.

After our first day visiting the plant, the entire team gathered back at the hotel to debrief. The conversation centered on labor relations. A number of the team members were enthusiastic about the exceptional degree of labor–management cooperation that we had observed. People cited examples at all levels of the operation—from the joint handling of grievances to the joint development of training to the facilitywide joint committees. Enthusiasm was building among members of the group. There was a real sense that we had seen evidence of an exceptional labor–management relationship.

All during the discussion, one group member—who had prior experience as an elected union official—remained silent. Finally, the group, expecting enthusiastic agreement, turned to this person. There was a crushing moment when she instead expressed serious concerns about what we had seen. Dramatic as the joint activities were, she said she was not sure they would be sufficient to deal with the challenges facing a union–management relationship in this context.

After an extended silence, we began to explore the potential limits or tensions that still existed in this setting. For example, it was clear that these parties were attempting to build a partnership where there was no clear model. Also, the two parent corporations—GM and Toyota—and the international union all viewed what was taking place from very different perspectives. As our discussion unfolded, we began to appreciate that the terms "adversarial" and "enterprise" only served to reinforce a polarized view about what was taking place at NUMMI—without fully capturing the complex and unfolding nature of this labor–management relationship.

Building on the conversation at NUMMI, we began to reflect on labor–management relations in all of our sites. This revealed a further limit with the terms since they were not helpful at all in organizing our thinking about labor relations in the nonunion organizations. Ultimately, we have turned to the anthropology literature for a set of terms that characterize reciprocal relationships and better match what we have seen.

Two more helpful terms are "symmetrical" and "complementary."[13] These terms are somewhat analogous to "adversarial" and "enterprise." The term "symmetrical" reflects a set of relations akin to bluffing—moves and countermoves that are mutually reinforcing. Symmetrical relationships are characterized by the dynamics of competition and escalation. The term "complementary" also refers to a reciprocal relationship but with connotations of interdependency, cooperation, and the building of constructive relations.

Instead of being institutional labels, the terms "symmetrical" and "complementary" refer to patterns of interaction. The patterns are reciprocal in both cases but rooted in different underlying assumptions. In a symmetrical relationship, the assumption is one of conflicting interests. In a complementary relationship, the assumption is one of common interests. The roles under each type of relationship are very different, reflecting these different underlying assumptions.

While a relationship may be primarily symmetrical in nature, it can have some complementary patterns as well. Similarly, a relationship that is dominantly complementary may still have some symmetrical dynamics. For example, the union–management relationship at NUMMI is primarily complementary, but there are symmetrical dynamics. As the vice president of human resources, Bill Childs, stated it, "While it is impossible for management and labor to always agree and always share the exact same goals, it is vital that management seek to enlarge the common ground which it shares with labor and to foster an understanding that labor and management have common responsibilities and a shared destiny."

The limits of the complementary relationship were illustrated on the issue of health and safety during a new model ramp-up. The complementary patterns were not sufficient to address a set of pressing ergonomic issues. When the union instead went to the state OSHA board, it set in motion a set of parallel, symmetrical responses by NUMMI to avoid censure. In this legalistic process, the parties returned to traditional adversarial roles, whose interaction routinely require the intervention of a referee. Importantly, however, the next model change was approached by both parties in a complementary problem-solving way that has served to reinvigorate both sides' commitment to working together.

The terms "complementary" and "symmetrical" apply equally as well to the nonunion sites. For example, at Ogihara there was tension around a proposal to use rotating shifts. This proposal, developed by management, reflected the common scheduling patterns in Japan. It was based on the view that rotating shifts was "fair" since everyone would share the burden.[14] The issue triggered a set of symmetrical dynamics in which employees began to circulate petitions protesting the idea. A set of town meetings was held to address the tension. Ultimately, management abandoned the proposal and maintained shift selection on the basis of seniority.

Based on this experience and other similar issues, management at Ogihara has considered establishing a facilitywide problem-solving forum. The latest news we had was that the company was in the process of considering possible mechanisms. We assume the aim is to develop a more complementary way of dealing with issues of fairness in the workplace.

The mechanisms used in a complementary relationship depend on intangible elements such as trust, shared information, values, and knowledge base. For example, the handling of grievances at NUMMI depends on joint investigation and data collection, both of which drive complementary problem solving. By contrast, grievance or complaint procedures in a symmetrical relationship are more likely to depend on tangible explicit knowledge, written contracts and policy statements, precedent, and legal roles.

It remains to be seen whether or not the terms "symmetrical" and "complementary" prove useful beyond the organizations we have examined. We are confident, however, that our search for these terms reflects the inadequacy of "adversarial" and "enterprise" for discussing labor relations in unionized and nonunion knowledge-driven operations.

Tangible to Intangible

Just as we wanted to discuss labor relations using the more expressive terms "symmetrical" and "complementary," we also view the labor relations process through the lens of tangible and intangible factors. In the current debate over labor relations in a lean production setting, critics use a symmetrically based set of intangibles to describe the work settings. For example, Fucini and Fucini describe life in the Flat Rock Mazda plant. They use words like "corporatewide antagonism" and "disillusioned" to illustrate their point.[15] In our view, these authors are writing from a symmetrical point of view and have their ideas shaped by the intangibles that accompany this perspective—intangibles such as distrust, suspicion, and anger. All of these are justified in a workplace where the management believes that asking workers not to think is a welcome part of a job. Henry Ford reflects this type of management attitude when he says,

> Of necessity, the work of an individual must be repetitive—not otherwise can he gain effortless speed which makes low prices and earns high wages. Some of our tasks are exceedingly monotonous . . . but then, also, many minds are monotonous—many men want to earn a living without thinking, and for these men a task which demands no brain is a boon.[16]

This view of workers has been changing over time as more and more employers become aware of the value of the knowledge that workers bring to their jobs. Unions have struggled for years to protect this knowledge through job classification and increased workplace dignity. The shift in the appreciation and value of worker knowledge requires a change in the structures and processes in order to maximize the value that all parties in the workplace receive. Another way of describing this is the shift from workers as interchangeable parts on the assembly line to pivotal elements of a knowledge-driven organization.

Knowledge is one intangible that has begun to assume greater and greater importance. Kaizen is one of the elements of a knowledge-driven workplace that must be considered from a labor relations perspective. We believe that the existence of such a system forces or indicates a change in workplace assumptions about roles, values, and behaviors of all parties. For example, the grievance procedure was used in a traditional labor relations setting to bring noncontractual as well as contractual problems to management's attention. Workers were limited in their ability to make changes in their workplaces in other ways. However, the kaizen-teian system explicitly values workers' tacit knowledge and allows mechanisms to alter both contractual and noncontractual aspects of the workplace.

In some organizations, the implementation of kaizen is blocked by fears of layoffs. In sites where the kaizen is most successful, the workforce has a stronger sense of employment security. Employers who implement kaizen most successfully understand and value the tacit knowledge of the individual employee. This understanding provides the basis for a union bargaining position that argues for employment security. The existence of employment security changes the bargaining goals of a union.

But the issue goes beyond substantive employment security provisions in a contract. As we saw in chapter 7, this necessary complement to kaizen cannot just be granted in a contract. It must be constructed over time through test events that shape a social contract. In a complementary relationship there will be an intangible but crucial process in which parties demonstrate and feel a shared responsibility for constructing systems that support kaizen as well as employment security. In a symmetrical relationship, the emphasis on tangible elements of the relationship can produce comparable contract language, but not the same outcomes.

In knowledge-driven work systems, collective bargaining issues are shifting to a greater emphasis on the intangible elements that shape the workplace. For these knowledge-driven production systems to function most effectively, people in those systems must accept and understand their interdependencies. It is impossible to maintain the traditional position that the parties have great independence and can walk away from the table or job to assert their rights. Walking away or disrupting the flow of work causes more than a stop in production; it causes an irreparable gap in the stream of knowledge and information that drives work. This is a change in intangible elements of the work relationship.

Union officials who understand labor issues, the contract, and manufacturing find themselves facing new decision points. For example, they can become facilitators of the manufacturing and kaizen processes. On the other hand, they can use the leverage created by the production system to drive the development of new union strategies and structures. Consider the case of the UAW at AAI. This story is one illustration of the opportunities and challenges that now exist for unions within new work organization systems.

As we described earlier, the conflict that arose as the plant was ramping up during one of Michigan's hottest summers caused a long-standing and bitter split in the labor relations. Nonetheless, it is important to recognize that experience at AAI is still characterized by a great deal of innovation and change. The union local is experimenting with nontraditional organizing campaigns with suppliers. Its success is a product of what it has learned from working in a lean manufacturing operation. In an interview, Phil Keeling, the UAW local president, told us, "Our members are not like other members—they've had the Mazda orientation—it impacts on the members' attitudes." He went on to discuss the organizing drives that the local had successfully undertaken at supplier firms.

> Our members and our leadership won with a good presence. The hierarchy [UAW] can't relate to this labor force. They are still playing the political appointments and the politics game. We know that to organize these people we must be completely honest and understand what life is like in the plant. We don't promise them the traditional money, we promise them a contract.

Management appears to be trying to build employee involvement independently without union support. In these regards, the situation is more complex than a traditional adversarial relationship. It seems to us that the intangible aspects are shaping the tangible.

The interplay between tangible and intangible aspects of labor relations is further complicated by the overlay of a cross-cultural dimension. For example, in discussing the contract ratification process, one manager described how his Japanese counterpart snatched a "vote no" sign off the wall, saying that it was not cooperative: "I said that snatching it off the wall makes it worse, but it took three hours for us each to try and understand." Here there is the very tangible manifestation of internal union politics—a "vote no" sign—interacting with a highly intangible Japanese sensibility about harmony and cooperation. The incident raises the question of how people in highly interdependent work systems can learn to handle intense internal disagreements.

It is imperative that people in the union and management understand the fundamental tensions and dilemmas of labor issues as well as have expertise in manufacturing practices. These individuals are central to the successful organizations that we saw. They also have interpersonal skills that are vital to their success in process facilitation. They incorporate, in effect, a combination of tangible and intangible skills and characteristics. Due to the nature of the labor relations environment, this is a different combination of skills than in the past.

Beyond Role Ambiguity

Studying Japanese-affiliated organizations provides us with a mirror through which we can view developments in North America. Instead of working from a blueprint of a Japanese model, many of these organizations are creating a new and distinctly North American approach to labor relations. Constraints within national legal systems demand that labor relations have to be different. For example, the types of complementary interactions found in Japan's enterprise system of unionism can only be approximated under U.S. law.

Across North America, the need for reexamination of union and management roles is increasingly surfacing as a result of shifts in work practices, the competitive environment, and new relational dynamics. It reflects the greater emphasis on intangible elements of the workplace. As these relationships are reexamined and co-evolve, all the stakeholders suffer varying degrees of role ambiguity and dissonance.[17] In the unionized Japanese-affiliated enterprises, the ambiguity is compounded because the implications are different depending on whether the organization features a traditional work system or a knowledge-driven system.

The ambiguity constrains leadership and reflects a harsh reality. Many of the historic sources of power and established norms are not effective in the ways they once were. Thus, union leaders who follow the same patterns of behavior that were once effective encounter unexpected and even opposite outcomes. For example, strong militancy expressed through traditional, more tangible tactics such as job actions (strikes, slowdowns, etc.) that could affect the quality of the product may result in union leaders being blamed for lost jobs or reduced productivity. At the same time, close working relationships demanded by joint processes may result in the perception that union leaders are "in bed with management."

In two of the organizations we studied, AAI and Hitachi Magnetics, we observed sharp swings in union election results: leadership slates elected on cooperative platforms were replaced by slates elected on adversarial platforms. In this regard, union leaders became captive to a larger dynamic of whether their interests and those of their members are better served by traditional adversarial relationships or by forging new joint cooperative labor–management alliances. For example, Phil Keeling at UAW Local 3000 was asked about contract negotiations and spoke of wanting "to go to the table with the gun loaded." He felt that a good sense of local solidarity had helped to convince AAI management to bargain a good contract. It is easy to see how using this terminology— "adversarial" versus "cooperative"—helps to create options that are not likely to be satisfactory for management, the union, or the membership. Further, framed this way, conflicting interests between union leaders and their members are accentuated.

This dynamic was evident at Hitachi, for example. New, younger union leaders were elected to office in the UAW local. The new leadership agreed to explore a joint relationship with management in response to economic pressures on the company. A joint labor-management committee was established and, after information sharing in this forum, the parties agreed to reopen negotiations to discuss health care costs. When this issue was brought before the rank and file for approval, it was voted down.

In this case, neither the union's nor the management's leadership recognized the importance of a process of education and communication necessary to enable union members to make decisions in a very competitive environment. Without access to an ongoing flow of critical information, the members of the local did not share the same urgency to change the contract that the union and management leadership did. In effect, they became a constraint on the actions of union and management leaders as they attempted to try new forms of labor relations.

Pressures from role ambiguity are often strongest on those groups of employees, both union and management, who understand the need to change or are caught in a set of circumstances that are created by the need to change. Organizational patterns frequently adapt more slowly than the perceptions of individuals who have access to the most information and must utilize that information in decision making. More pressure is created when those individuals do not have the authority or ability to make change happen. It is also possible that these individuals cannot change others in their respective organizations due to lack of communication skills or opportunities.

There is always ambiguity in being a union leader. Additional ambiguity arises from a clash between relatively static organizational systems and changing contextual circumstances. For example, in such systems it is difficult to respond to shifts in the demographics of the membership or societal changes that represent sources of tension in a democratic organization such as a union. Additionally, where competitive pressures increase, such as we saw at Hitachi, the ambiguity is amplified since the work system is less able to respond to the changed competitive context. Instead, union members are pushed to work harder in the existing system and the union leadership feels unable to make constructive efforts on behalf of the members. Further complicating the situation is the awareness on the part of these union leaders and their members of many innovative experiments occurring in North America and elsewhere in the world. Thus, they know that their present system is not working as it should, yet neither they nor their members are sufficiently part of efforts to construct a new system.

In those settings where the principles of knowledge-driven work are effectively and systematically implemented, additional forms of ambiguity emerge. The frustration level may be equally high for union leaders in less knowledge-driven settings, but the implications for action are different. In a knowledge-driven system that is functioning effectively, a new source of ambiguity for union leaders concerns the existence of many viable channels by which members' problems are solved. When workers are taught problem-solving methods, they may have less need for a traditional grievance procedure. Greater independent problem-solving capability can translate to less reliance on stewards as well as supervisors. This also means that the types of issues that are then brought to the union are very different. One example is the disputes that arise over team leader selection.

The experience at AAI illustrates this situation. The union challenged management's selection of team leaders, which had been imported as one of many elements of an imposed lean production system. Based on this challenge, new contract language was negotiated that allows for the election of team leaders.

Now, however, there is a new dilemma. How can a union leader respond when she receives complaints over the actions of a team leader elected by the team who are also union members? Since AAI is set up to be a knowledge-driven system, yet has a more symmetrical union–management relationship, this is a very complicated situation. Either the union must pick and choose among contending union members, or it must abandon the issue, leaving it for management to resolve, or the union can join with management and coordinate a response, driving it toward a more complementary relationship.

A second source of ambiguity concerns the degree to which union members apply the same principles in their union activities as they do on the job. For example, Phil Keeling, president of UAW Local 3000 at AAI, commented that members would use the same problem-solving language from their team training to tackle issues such as how the local union spent their dues.

A third source of ambiguity arises in the context of collective bargaining and contract administration. Like managers, union representatives find their traditional authority questioned and challenged by members who take the allocation of power in the workplace very seriously. The logic of a conventionally negotiated contractual relationship can constrain rather than enable workers to resolve problems. It is a serious dilemma for a union representative to discover that the best solution to a problem is a violation of the contract. One illustration of this can be seen in events at NUMMI in which limits to transfer rights across work areas were negotiated in order to maximize the benefits of cross training in a team-based work system.

A fourth source of ambiguity lies at a strategic level. The very existence of these workplaces is a result of strategic investment decisions and joint venture agreements. Consequently, there is always the possibility of future strategic shifts. For example, the joint venture between GM and Toyota was sanctioned by the Federal Trade Commission. The order signed in 1984 limited production to small cars due to protests at that time from other major U.S. car producers. Both partners eventually became dissatisfied with the limitations of the agreement and threatened to close the plant if the restrictions were not lifted. The agreement was renewed but could have ended or been modified.[18] While GM has chosen to remain a partner in this case, Toyota is taking on an increasingly dominant role in the partnership. This means that the UAW must consider the implications of an ongoing partnership in which Toyota is the principal counterpart. It also creates new tensions and opportunities in relations with the rest of the UAW–GM system. Similarly, these settings are particularly susceptible to global developments such as shifts in the yen-dollar exchange rate, governmental trade negotiations, and global business policies within the corporations.

Finally, incomplete understanding of the differences and similarities between U.S. and Japanese unions creates ambiguity. Union leaders in the United States perceive the enterprise union model in Japan as similar to company unions that have existed in the United States. They are surprised to discover that Japanese unions do not meekly follow the lead of their managers and have created workplaces in which their members have great impact. In fact, Japanese unions are representational organizations in a distinctive way that matches their culture and context. It is not clear to most American observers that labor relations in Japan start from a different set of assumptions. One of those assumptions is the unquestioned legitimacy of the union.

There is real tension concerning the degree to which a U.S. union dealing with a Japanese parent company will end up moving toward an enterprise structure, continue the symmetrical behaviors of the U.S. system, or develop some new complementary structure that is different from all of those. When companies come to this country, the relationships they develop with their employees—and, where they exist, the organizations that represent these employees—can be the cause of tremendous uncertainty. This uncertainty is a root of ambiguity that will drive change. The people in these dilemmas will shape the outcomes through the strength of their will, their knowledge, and the interdependence of their interests.

The Shift in Labor Relations

Labor relations as we observed them in our knowledge-driven sites facilitate the constructive use of the knowledge of the workforce. While we believe this is essential in an environment where the primary sources of competitive advantage are quality, innovation, and flexibility, it may not be universal practice. Although we have suggested new terms to describe what we believe is a shift in labor relations, adversarial relations still dominate U.S. labor relations.

Now management and union leaders in knowledge-driven sites are discovering that collective bargaining must consider different details. These details reflect the new importance of the minds and skills of the laborers in the development of each organization and help it to adapt to the changes in the environment. Management can no longer rely on a constant flow of new people who will learn the basics of a job defined in Tayloristic terms. Unions may find themselves in the dilemma of undoing many principles that they developed over years of bargaining but that now have become constraints. In an environment where work rules are written to allow greater flexibility, the relationships are built on different, intangible foundations. For example, there must be a recognition of union legitimacy, vigilance in the care and shaping of trust is essential, and the parties must begin to consider the greater depth of shared interests between them.

Where we observed labor relations responding to new production and management systems, changes to work rules also meant changes in the expectations and relationships throughout the organization. For example, employment security is one of the prerequisites for relationships in which people must be willing to take new risks, acquire new competencies, and use those skills to push the organization forward. In organizations in which perceptions of employment security are tenuous, workers are mainly concerned with individual interests rather than organizationally based interests.

In the nonunionized sites that we visited, patterns of relations are developing without the guidelines and constraints of previous language. This allows for greater shifts in workplace activities but also reduces the potential number, credibility, and collective impact of mechanisms available to employers to establish a flow of information in the workplace. In an era in which the rapid flow of information and knowledge adds to an organization's competitiveness, strength will be found in the ability to facilitate this process. Organizations that understand this knowledge-creation dynamic have the potential for great success in today's global environment.

Of all the topics covered in this book, the relationship between knowledge-driven work and labor relations has been the most difficult to write about. There are many more puzzles than answers in the practices that we observed. We found terms such as "adversarial" and "enterprise labor relations" overly simplistic. Traditional union and nonunion distinctions were not as helpful in accounting for the diversity of practices in comparison to distinctions based on the way knowledge is valued. We hope the new terms that we have begun to use—"symmetrical" and "complementary"—capture some aspects of the emerging realities or fuel further dialogue about what terms to use. While it is clear that knowledge-driven work poses many difficult challenges for the institutions associated with collective interests in the workplace, it remains to be seen how these challenges will ultimately be resolved.

9

Implications

· ·

During our visits to the organizations discussed in this book, we continually met people whose work and personal lives were changing in fundamental ways. Driving the changes were the many aspects of diffusion and knowledge creation. These words—"diffusion" and "knowledge creation"—are our words, not necessarily the words that would be used by the people we met. From them, we mostly heard about the process of change—working, interacting, and even thinking in new ways. Most striking was that many of these people reported with great conviction that they were creating a better way of working.

Creating knowledge-driven workplaces that can elicit such responses requires leadership. Leadership must exist at all levels and support alternative ways of thinking about the concepts of knowledge, trust, inclusion, and power. Each of these factors influences the roles that people play in the workplace. We found ourselves forced to redefine the concept of leadership based on the new dimensions of these roles. Conventional notions of leadership do not match the realities emerging in some of the worksites we visited. The implications of our research involve changes in how people see themselves, including people who have not traditionally thought of themselves as leaders, as well as those who have traditionally expected to be the only leaders.

What Do We Mean by Implications?

In this changing environment, writing a chapter on implications poses several distinct responsibilities. For a point made in the preceding eight chapters to become an implication, it must meet several stringent tests.

First, an implication must stand out. It must register to the observer as some kind of a marked environmental change or variation. We were surprised by our reactions to situations as diverse as immaculate, well-organized factory floors, visibly appealing and informationally dense worksites, union leaders and plant managers in identical company uniforms, innovative and efficient parts presentations, cafeterias that served hamburgers with tonkatsu sauce, and the obvious pleasure with which people spoke about their enterprises. We were also troubled by factors like the dashed expectations of workers who felt that initial promises weren't kept, the slowness of developing shared values, and the potential for pain that faces workers in an intense work environment. Each variation or surprise is a potential source of implications in a general sense.

As the shock of a change or discrepancy registers, the second requirement for it to become an implication is that the observer understands why he or she noticed this particular variation. We react to material we read because we see it as confirming other information we know. Newly noticed information that is novel and not obvious extends our previous thinking. We internalize these points because they appear to clarify our thinking or cause us dissonance. The most powerful implications possess the power to force us to react to them or categorize them in some way.

Once information is registered and categorized, the third process that must occur is that the observer must filter it through his or her experience base to assess whether it adds practical value. Within seconds, observers will make judgments as to whether this new information has the capacity to encourage them to reconceptualize their prior ways of thinking and truly stimulate thought as an implication.

Finally, an implication has to be something worth incorporating into our thoughts and actions. For example, reading a book is something that we usually do alone, but the application of what we read involves reflection and, often, exploration with others. Given the importance that we give to the concept of virtual knowledge, it should come as no surprise that we welcome and even urge such reflection and analysis.

Implications for Leaders

This final chapter offers a way of rethinking leadership that takes into account the many lessons we have learned about global diffusion and knowledge-driven work systems. Models of leadership differ greatly within the traditional and the knowledge-driven firm. The traditional leadership style forces the leader to continually enhance and upgrade his or her individual skills. Leadership styles observed in new work systems demand that the leader develop the skills of the group more strongly. As we considered implications for leadership, our research team came face to face with the need to see leadership as rooted in a very different sense of self and relationships.

Essentially, implications for our readers will be drawn from four areas that we believe stand out after our 5-year journey. These implications are, by definition, four dimensions of leadership and must be considered before taking action to restructure organizations to better incorporate virtual knowledge. The four main implication areas we will be discussing are knowledge, inclusion, trust, and power/influence.

Knowledge

We have discovered that intangibles predict the incorporation of tangible knowledge in diffusion processes. Consider, for example, andon systems, a tangible aspect of lean production systems that is widely copied and diffused. These involve large electronic boards mounted near the ceiling (to be visible from many parts of an operation) with lights indicating the status of various machines and the production levels. Linked to the boards are buttons or cords that employees can use to call for help (green lights change to yellow) or to halt production (yellow lights change to red). The installation of this sort of system does not automatically instill the ability or motivation to use it appropriately. The lights and numbers might be there, but they will not be used without attention to intangibles such as trust, kaizen-driven learning, and commitment.

Intangibles such as trust, kaizen, and commitment are quite complex. They may be hard to see or touch, but they are essential if people are to generate knowledge through problem-solving skills and other mechanisms. Thus, intangible factors activate willingness to collaborate at all levels.[1] Consequently, attention to intangibles is essential.

Collaboration unleashes tacit knowledge and produces an alignment of intangibles and tacit knowledge. This alignment enables organizations to perceive ideas as opportunities and to reconceptualize explicit knowledge and tangible innovations into a productive arrangement for the enterprise. Continuous information sharing across groups and levels enables this valuable alignment process to constantly focus everyone on the relevant issues. This alignment of tacit knowledge, focused on shared goals, enables the phenomenon we call virtual knowledge. Leaders must create environments where tacit knowledge is valued. Providing a vision and encouraging interaction that brings out knowledge in ways that build shared values are important leadership tasks.

For traditional leaders, the goal may have been facilitating efforts at organizational change through the alignment of explicit knowledge and tangibles. We predict that focusing only on explicit knowledge and tangibles is doomed to fail. Trust, loyalty to company goals, learning, and employment security are powerful intangibles when coupled with stakeholder motivation to surface and channel their tacit knowledge. Putting these comments about knowledge into a work systems framework may prove helpful in understanding their implications for today's organizations.

For much of the twentieth century, mass production served as the dominant paradigm. It offered a clear model for the use of knowledge. Valued knowledge was possessed by executives, but especially those in what Henry Mintzberg calls the "technostructure."[2] The technostructure was composed of people such as staff specialists in manufacturing engineering, industrial engineering, plant layout engineering, cost accounting, labor relations, and production control. These experts used specialized knowledge to standardize the work of factory operators who were actually responsible for producing goods and services.

As we noted earlier, knowledge possessed by workers, union leaders, support staff, and those not in managerial or technical elites was considered to be inconsequential. Sociotechnical systems gained credibility in the 1970s and 1980s because they offered a way to tap employees' explicit and tacit knowledge regarding quality, safety, and other aspects of operations. In the 1980s and 1990s, lean production systems also tapped employee knowledge but linked this to ways to reduce inefficiency and waste. This core principle of reducing waste was accomplished by changing an organization's perception of employee knowledge and the presence of enhanced information-sharing mechanisms. People were now valued for their brains as well as their hands. Knowledge-driven work systems, including more advanced forms of lean manufacturing and STS, have expanded the knowledge-generating role of all employees to create organizations with greater capacity to handle change and cross-cultural diffusion.

Workers with experience in mass production find it difficult to believe managerial statements that it is not only acceptable to stop the line but required to increase organizational performance. It will help to return to our example of the andon board at the beginning of this section. Lacking intangible factors such as trust, no one on the line feels empowered to use the andon system. Thus the system that is intended to energize worker problem solving and to tap into explicit and tacit knowledge becomes a symbol of the failure to generate adequate workplace trust.

Understanding the roles played by tacit and explicit knowledge in the innovation and diffusion process is one major insight of our writing. Understanding that involvement in knowledge generation is one of the major aspects of diffusion is a second major implication. Linking knowledge generation and inclusion comes next.

Inclusion

The established theories of leadership are often called "situation" theories. These theories state that interaction between leaders, followers, and situational contingencies determine the "right" leadership style. Our extension of leadership theory is not a quest for some new "style." Rather, we have observed that anyone could be a leader at any time—at least in some of the organizations we studied. Executives did indeed offer leadership visions and suggestions for action in the sites we observed, but so did workers, union leaders, team leaders, and managers at various levels.

Everyone leads in a knowledge-driven work system. New designs, new production requirements, and cultural anomalies are all approached by teamwork and by focus on sharing information. Ideas and perceptions are discussed until gut-level issues are explored and realistic options for handling the situation are generated and understood. A crucial point here is the value of all the knowledge generated.[3]

Discussions are not, however, democratic in the sense that everyone has a vote or a veto. Formal leaders can and do convey urgency; they definitely shape and move the agenda. However, their leadership skill is reflected particularly in the way they respect and empower their co-workers or team members to bring their best ideas and concerns to situations affecting their work lives.

Our second insight is that members at all levels of the organization generate knowledge. We recognize the implications of the power of inclusion. Although it is an intangible factor, it brings tacit and explicit knowledge to bear in modern work systems.

Trust and Interdependence

Our third implication is the power of trust in supporting other intangibles, which in turn enables tangible factors of a diffused idea or change to be accepted and implemented successfully. We have learned about the importance of building trust from many years of listening to workplace vignettes. We shall try to be straightforward.

- Trust is the emotional gatekeeper that determines whether any individual or team member will generate or share knowledge.

- Without trust, aligned tacit knowledge and virtual knowledge will not be present.

- Faith in the ultimate success of the idea or the enterprise is interwoven with trust.

- Faith is trust in events not seen.

- Trust is based on shared experiences, behaviors, stories, and problem solving. Like virtual knowledge, it comes from interdependence but is a precursor to sharing.

- Trust and interdependence are closely related. The organization's main resource for addressing ambiguity and change is its ability to align tacit and explicit knowledge. These break down if parties do not trust each other.

Credibility and trust are critical intangible issues in designing modern production systems and in being able to learn from other systems. At first, we saw the critical issue of trust in the transplanted Japanese work systems as being culturally sensitive. Could Americans rely on Japanese methods? Could Japanese trust U.S.-based adaptations to their systems? Now we view trust as an integral part of any production system. How do people of both nationalities build organizations based in trust, understanding, and commitment to relationships with labor unions, suppliers, and communities?

The fundamental nature of trust was illustrated by one of our authors who had many years of experience in training supervisors and managers. In teaching leadership seminars in the late 1960s and 1970s, he noted that participants were almost always tremendously resistant to learning about leadership methods that created strong cohesive groups and encouraged knowledge generation by shop-floor workers. They preferred leadership models that favored "treating everyone as an individual." When shown how groups can use their knowledge to enhance quality, reduce waste, increase flexibility, and diminish absenteeism, participants simply said, "I believe you are right, but I cannot take that big a risk." They pointed out that cohesive groups may turn on them and present a solid front against the typical model of top-down imposed change. Since they could not trust upper management to stop using "the hammer," middle managers felt it was easier to impose change on isolated individuals than on cohesive and empowered groups and teams.

Another set of implications regarding trust contains themes from this story. Global markets, increased competition, rapid product-innovation cycles, global manufacturing, information technology advances, and new forms of work organization and production systems are present today. These changes require successful firms to generate and sustain innovation. Therefore, knowledge generation, inclusiveness, and trust, as well as related intangibles, such as creativity, cooperation, and courage, will be necessary for mutual leadership to occur. Mutual leadership is necessary to empower all stakeholders and to align knowledge in ways that are unique, discerned, and shared.

Yet leadership must be even more. Given the shifts around trust and interdependence, power and influence also play different roles in the equation. This next set of implications will address influence and power as we have come to understand them.

Influence and Power

In earlier discussions of implications, we wrote about mutual leadership. Mutual leadership emphasizes what we term influence processes. To derive implications, we view leadership as the process of influencing each stakeholder to share relevant tacit and explicit knowledge. If influence is a process, then power is a resource that enables leaders to encourage and empower employee knowledge generation and sharing.

Traditional leaders who resist empowering teams and groups stake their careers on their ability to lead by using one type of power. They count on using positional power or authority, the legitimate power delegated through the company hierarchy.[4] Positional power is the weakest of all power bases in generating knowledge. It leaves only the ability to manipulate people through the use of rewards and punishments. These power bases—positional, reward, and punishment—deny the opportunity to activate important intangibles. Trust, employment security, and the intangible factor of "the joy of work" gained from using one's valued skills are not realized.[5] The intrinsic excitement of contributing to an organization with which the person identifies is also lost. Adopting a leadership approach that fails to activate so many forms of knowledge generation makes little sense.

Expert power resides in everyone. We were told the following story by Michael Damer at NUMMI:

> A Toyota executive is on a plant tour surrounded by plant management and one subordinate determined to ingratiate himself with the executive. This subordinate frequently praised the executive's vision

and diligence as the tour progressed. Finally, the executive stopped and said, "What would happen if there were a tragedy and I had a heart attack right now?" Sensing a trap, the subordinate quickly responded that the executive had done an excellent job of building a succession plan. He said it would be difficult, but they would be able to continue operations. Then the executive pointed to a production worker actively performing tasks along an assembly line and asked, "What would happen if he were to stop doing his job right now?" The subordinate responded that production would have to stop immediately. Then the executive asked the key question: "Who is more important?"

The point was clear. The worker's contribution enabled the line to run that day, and the line produced the products the company needed to supply its markets. The power of leaders is greatest when it is used to empower others to use their expertise and knowledge, tacit and explicit, to help the company operate and adapt to changing realities.

This story poses important implications for the use of power in the influence process. A major source of power is knowledge and expertise. Explicit knowledge can be withheld at some risk, but tacit knowledge can be withdrawn and withheld without immediate notice. Our earlier implications held that the alignment of everyone's tacit knowledge with the organization's vision and direction is vital to the alignment of explicit knowledge. Therefore, it becomes obvious that only an empowering leader can foster the virtual knowledge that enables diffusion and reverse diffusion to occur. Our final set of implications regarding leadership is that the best leaders are those who know how to find, access, and harness tacit knowledge.

Denso U.S.A.'s third president, Mr. Mineo "Sam" Kawai, pointed out that appropriate management attitudes to subordinates are "difficult to explain to American managers." He stated, "It seems to me that management's attitude is basically that their responsibility is to achieve targets that are set." This, he pointed out, results in ever stronger pressure the lower the status of the manager. It also makes it harder for the lower-level managers to speak up if they feel that "the order is too tall." In contrast, he stated that "I personally believe that differences among people in terms of ability are quite limited." He observed that people are in superior positions for functional reasons, not because they are superior by nature. As a result, the more senior the manager, the more important it is to be humble and open to what others might say. He quoted a Japanese maxim that is often presented to those who are promoted—"The more ripe the rice, the lower its head."

The major implication here is that the knowledge-creation process must be understood as the engine driving modern organizations. The story is not yet fully understood, but the outline of answers is beginning to emerge from our implications summary.

Conundrums

In this final section of the chapter, we will review a number of puzzles, challenges, and dilemmas that are important and unresolved in our minds. These conundrums build on the concepts and insights that we have presented in the book while pointing the way for future scholarship and innovation in the field.

> *Why is it so hard in traditional organizations*
> *to foster an appreciation for the intangibles?*
> *Why don't more leaders "get it?"*

Leaders in most traditional organizations include among their objectives improving product or service quality, achieving continuous improvement in operations, generating innovations that provide opportunities for growth, and investing in employees as the most important asset. These "leaders" will launch or implement one or more programs designed to achieve these objectives. As we have already noted, the tangible elements of the programs and initiatives are not sufficient, yet leaders who benchmark some of the organizations in our study do not seem to understand or appreciate the intangibles.

Our preliminary conclusion is that the values and assumptions that underlie traditional work systems are remarkably well entrenched in many of our schools, communities, and workplaces. These notions of hierarchy and expert authority can even be found in many religious institutions and in aspects of our personal lives. This contrasts with the many people who told us how their lives had changed when they began working in some of the new work systems we studied. It is not clear that it is possible to appreciate or embrace the ideas merely by visiting or hearing about such systems.

This is, of course, a dilemma in writing a book such as this. Important parts of our learning happened as we incorporated the intangibles into the way we operate as a research team. It is for this reason that we have included our own experiences along these lines at various places in the book. Thus, one of our findings is that this final chapter should not represent a conclusion in any sense of the word. It should be a stimulus for experiments and learning.

*How do the dynamics between tangible and
intangible improvements unfold over time?*

We know from our field work that tangible improvements are made possible through a wide range of intangible contributions. We even have field data from one of the organizations we studied—Denso Manufacturing–Michigan, Inc.—that demonstrates a positive and significant relationship between intangible and tangible improvement suggestions. Still, there is much more to be learned.

For example, we know that certain tangible features of a work system are essential before other intangibles can come into play. No matter how committed people are to preventive maintenance principles in a manufacturing operation, the presence of a great deal of excess in-process inventory will make it hard to maintain discipline around these principles. Similarly, no matter how committed people are to the intangible of continuous learning, the lack of staffing levels or budget authorization to support training will undercut learning processes.

In this book, we have highlighted many of the intangibles that we see as most salient, including concepts such as virtual knowledge, kaizen-driven learning, leadership, trust, and interdependency. What we cannot do, based just on our data, is report on any particular sequences of tangible and intangible priorities to guide the implementation of a knowledge-driven work system. Instead, we point to a learning process that is essential to managing the ever-increasing interdependence among the intangibles and the tangibles. Perhaps the most important intangible in this context is the interdependence among the people who make products or deliver services and the people who support those on the front lines.

*What is the future for union and management leadership
when front-line workers are essential and building
ever-increasing capabilities?*

Fundamental changes in union and management organizations are required if knowledge-creation processes are to be valued and supported. These changes include abandoning the assumption that more senior or higher-level people are necessarily more expert in every issue.

At the same time, the presence of many more people able to implement change increases the need for standardization and leadership. There is a real tension here. How do you keep from stifling or squandering the great range of ideas that can emerge from knowledge-creation processes? This is a core tension between standardization and variation, and it requires leadership at all levels.

To lead people in a knowledge-driven work system requires mastering the delicate art of encouraging variation to emerge within a highly standardized framework. Moreover, it requires being comfortable with the inevitable reality that some of the variation will drive change in the framework itself. This applies to union leaders, management leaders, and others who are responsible for a system but learning that they depend on the knowledge of many people for the system to succeed. Incremental improvements can and will drive systems change, if people have the patience and courage to let it happen.

Can emerging social contracts in a select group of organizations survive and diffuse on a broader scale?

Clearly, some of the organizations that we studied are reaching into the larger communities where they are based and extending the concepts of continuous improvement. For example, we saw that Denso Manufacturing–Michigan, Inc., was devoting substantial resources to improving the quality of schools in the Battle Creek community.

At the same time, many more organizations are playing one community against another, extracting tax and training subsidies, and then moving on to the lowest bidder a few years later. This is a fundamental contradiction in a world where organizations are pursuing business strategies that are in many ways knowledge driven. If the organization is relying on the ideas and energies of its employees to support quality, continuous improvement, or innovation and it then disregards commitments to the communities in which these employees live, great social tension is inevitable.

This challenge is not limited to operations in the United States or Japan. It is a global issue. These new work systems not only build capability for improving workplace operations, they build capability for driving change at many levels in society.

Will the leading competitors in the next century be learning organizations able to manage the dynamics of global diffusion? Will they even be organizations that are with us today?

We have had the privilege of studying some companies that are leading examples in the diffusion of knowledge-driven work systems. Yet even in these organizations we found difficulty in managing all of the dynamics of diffusion. This was especially true with respect to reverse diffusion.

Simply stated, we have found that it is hard for teachers to become students. Yet the core lesson around knowledge-generating processes is that it is not possible to predict where the most important new ideas will emerge. To profit from the knowledge potential of a global workforce, they must be knowledge driven on a global basis.

How does an organization become truly knowledge driven? It does not happen through benchmarking focused on copying the tangibles. This will miss the intangibles and the essential nature of what we are calling virtual knowledge. Consider the comment of a Toyota official when asked by a U.S. union leader why they were willing to share so much information about what they do. The response was, "By the time you master what we are telling you today, we will be doing something very different."

It is the process of knowledge creation, not just the result, that drives continuous improvement. By now, it should be clear that becoming more knowledge driven produces powerful results, but it will also generate unintended consequences. People matter because they are the source of the knowledge, the only way the knowledge is applied, and, ultimately, the beneficiaries of the knowledge.

Virtual knowledge is a fragile foundation for the global diffusion of knowledge-driven work systems. It is fragile because it is both fleeting and dependent on leadership and trust. Though fragile, virtual knowledge is also potent. Shared understandings that result from these sorts of dialogue about new work systems represent the foundation for fundamental change in organizations and society.

As we look to the next century, we see an interweaving of the two forms of knowledge-driven work highlighted in this book—the STS and the lean manufacturing models. Organizations that have relied more on worker autonomy via the STS model are finding that increased interdependency and increased need to eliminate waste pushes them toward more of a lean production model. For example, the Saturn Corporation— a high-profile organization built on STS assumptions—is struggling to become more "lean." At the same time, organizations that have relied on more elimination of waste via the lean model are finding that increased attention to the STS forms of empowerment is essential. This is evident, for example, at Toyota's new Kyushu plant, where buffers have been added to the production system. This is aimed at giving teams more autonomy and reducing the intensity of work.

Even as we observe what seems to be a synthesis between the lean and STS forms of knowledge-driven work systems, our research on diffusion suggests that yet unknown models are sure to emerge. The question is not whether there will be continued variation in work systems. It is certain that this will happen. Rather, the question for the next century centers on whether we can fashion organizations that can learn to use and develop the knowledge of the people who work there.

The implications for matters such as leadership and trust that are outlined in this chapter build on long-standing themes in the literatures on work and organizations. How then do they fit in a book with a subtitle highlighting "unexpected" lessons? These findings stand out in the context of an increasingly global economy where observers in many different countries decry the erosion or collapse of social contracts in the workplace. Instead of seeing the global marketplace as only destroying notions of job security, continuous improvement, communications, trust, and collective representation in workplaces, we see a countervailing trend driven by the global diffusion of knowledge-driven work systems.

The diffusion of knowledge-driven work systems has generated many unexpected lessons for the workers, managers and representatives in these work places. We were unprepared for the degree to which we found that the global diffusion of such systems is both potent and fragile. Knowledge-driven work has the potential to transform both individuals and organizations.

To truly value and build on knowledge and capability at all levels requires a bold rethinking of every aspect of a work process. At the same time it requires humility in recognizing just how difficult this is to do and how dependent it is on people other than yourself. Being both bold and humble is essential for being knowledge driven and vital when helping people to work together across cultures.

Notes

• •

Chapter 1

1. More information on the Work Practices Diffusion Team can be found in the preface.

2. Lessons from exchanges between North America and Japan have implications for the many companies from around the world seeking to establish new operations in China, Southeast Asia, the former Soviet republics, South America, and Africa. Indeed, these lessons even have implications for the movement of innovative practices across regions or organizational subcultures within an organization—in the public or private sectors. In each case, the diffusion of innovation depends on the constructive channeling of the virtual knowledge generated around the proposed new practices.

3. This hints at a sense of vulnerability, which may be disconcerting to many who normally think of work in very tangible terms. Throughout this book we will discuss the dynamic tension created by the juxtaposition of tangible and intangible. The notion of fragile was borrowed from a 1986 unpublished paper by Haruo Shimada and John Paul MacDuffie "Industrial Relations and 'Humanware'" (p. 27). These authors explain that the system will not work on its own without human actions.

4. See, for example, Peter Drucker, *Post-Capitalist Society* (New York: Harper Business, 1993); Ikujiro Nonaka and Hirotaka Takeuchi, *The Knowledge-Creating Company: How Japanese Companies Create the Dynamics of Innovation* (New York: Oxford University Press, 1995); Julian E. Orr, *Talking about Machines: An Ethnography of a Modern Job* (Ithaca, N.Y.: Cornell University Press, 1995); Jean Lave, *Cognition in Practice* (Cambridge: Cambridge University Press, 1988); Robert E. Cole, *Strategies for Learning: Small-Group Activities in American, Japanese, and Swedish Industry* (Berkeley: University of California Press, 1989); W. Edward Deming, *Out of Crisis* (Cambridge, Mass.: Center for Advanced Engineering Study, Massachusetts Institute of Technology, 1986); Paul S. Adler, "The Learning Bureaucracy: New

163

United Motor Manufacturing, Inc." *Research in Organizational Behavior* 1, (1993):111–194.

5. Karl E. Weick, *Sensemaking in Organizations* (Thousand Oaks, Calif.: Sage Publications, 1995).

6. We will show that workers are a vital component of the success of Japanese industry. This idea is not addressed in *The Machine That Changed the World* by James P. Womack, Daniel T. Jones, and Daniel Roos (New York: Macmillan, 1990).

7. There is some irony in the fact that our study started with $500 in contrast to the $5 million that our MIT colleagues were privileged to have.

8. Mike Parker and M. Jane Slaughter, *Choosing Sides: Unions and the Team Concept* (Boston: South End Press, 1988).

9. In-process product inventories are stockpiles of material that build up between stations in a production process. In many traditional auto parts and assembly plants, it is typical to have as much as 3 or 4 days of in-process inventory on hand at each stage of production. In Japanese or U.S. facilities operating according to lean production principles, 2 to 3 hours of in-process inventory or even "level production" with continuous transfers is more typical.

10. Thomas Kochan, Harry Katz, and Robert McKersie, *The Transformation of American Industrial Relations* (New York: Basic Books, 1986).

11. Furthermore, we understood that Japan experienced a period of conflict among government, management, and labor in the 1950s that led to an undermining of independent communist-led unions. These unions were replaced, with support by General MacArthur during the postwar reconstruction in Japan, with the more familiar enterprise union model that now characterizes Japanese private-sector industrial relations. Yet this enterprise model did not extend to the public sector in Japan. Thus, we knew that overly simplified views of unions in Japan would not be helpful in understanding the handling of union–management relations in North American locations. Also, the interweaving of U.S. influence on Japanese practices a half-century ago represents a precursor of the cross-cultural transfers that we are now studying.

12. Jeremiah J. Sullivan, *Invasion of the Salarymen: The Japanese Business Presence in America* (Westport, Conn.: Praeger, 1992); Robert Perrucci, "Cultural Integration," in the proceedings of "Global Partners, Local Communities and Japanese Transplants," a conference sponsored by Illinois Wesleyan University and the Japan Foundation Center for Global Partnership (Bloomington: Illinois Wesleyan University, October, 1992).

13. Dr. Iwao Ishino reported this fact from a guest lecture at Michigan State University by Dr. Nancy Henninger Reisig, formerly the director of the Michigan liaison office in Tokyo. This research group met Dr. Reisig when she arranged our visit at the Mazda plant in Flat Rock.

14. See Robert J. Thomas, *What Machines Can't Do: Politics and Technology in the Industrial Enterprise* (Berkeley: University of California Press, 1994); and Robert Ozaki, *Human Capitalism: The Japanese Enterprise System as World Model* (New York: Penguin Books, 1991).

15. Our incorporation of anthropology reflects the broader multidisciplinary orientation of the project. We were honored to be recognized for our work along these lines in the form of the 1994 MSU Phi Kappa Phi Honor Society Award for Excellence in Interdisciplinary Scholarship.

16. The cross-cultural perspective hit a resonant chord within the group, given that nine nationalities were represented among the 12 project members. We organized ourselves in ways that harnessed that diversity productively and led us to spend many hours clarifying and defining terms. We were fairly quick to reject monolithic views of U.S. and Japanese cultures because so many of us were in the midst of a cross-cultural adaptation process in our own graduate education. For those of us who had not come to MSU from abroad, the seminar led us into an equivalent cross-cultural experience.

Ultimately, this changed our lives and directly affected in countless ways our life here at MSU and even among a mix of colleagues and practitioners around the world. For example, some class members were also working as employees or consultants to change initiatives in the field, and these were shaped in dramatic ways as a result of our shared experiences.

17. The idea of unintended consequences builds directly on a reading of Andrew M. Scott's book, *The Dynamics of Interdependence* (Chapel Hill: University of North Carolina Press, 1982, pp. 12–25). Scott is concerned with the communication and diffusion of the global system and economy. The concept of unintended consequences is particularly relevant when one tries to anticipate both the long- and short-term results of a diffusion program. Anticipating the outcome of an innovation in one's own culture is difficult enough, but trying to guess what it may be in a culture different from our own involves greater risks and uncertainties. In the present study, we did not try to anticipate the consequences, but rather attempted to document as clearly as we could some of the key events or outcomes that were not anticipated. Perhaps in future studies, documentary evidence of this kind may be helpful in avoiding some of the undesirable side effects of a diffusion program.

18. A Smithsonian presentation on the influence of Columbus's arrival in the New World entitled "The Seeds of Change: A Quincentennial Commemoration" (1991) prompted our first working title for this book—the seeds of change—which reflected our growing focus on cross-cultural diffusion. The focus has remained, but the book's final title reflects our belief in the crucial role of people and knowledge in today's workplaces.

19. As a further contribution to cross-cultural diffusion, our group took on the great responsibility for closely assessing these comparative culinary issues in the various plant cafeterias. In part, this reflected unintended learning on our part regarding the importance of food for sustaining research of this kind.

20. See Anthony Giddens, *Social Theory and Modern Sociology* (Stanford, Calif.: Stanford University Press, 1987).

21. See Anselm L. Strauss, *Negotiations: Varieties, Contexts, Processes, and Social Order* (San Francisco: Jossey-Bass, 1978).

22. See Richard Walton, Joel Cutcher-Gershenfeld, and Robert McKersie, *Strategic Negotiations: A Theory of Change in Labor–Management Relations* (Boston: Harvard Business School Press, 1994).

23. In Japan there is a relatively well-established set of social understandings around what some have termed the core and periphery workforces. While there is some tension in Japan regarding this division in the workforce, it is still modest compared to the lack of shared understandings in the United States.

24. During the course of this project, some members of our research team introduced concepts of systems thinking to the group—even though our initial focus was not driven by systems theory. In particular, our reading from the emerging literatures on complex adaptive systems and large-scale systems change gave us a helpful set of tools to aid our understanding of what we were observing.

In our fieldwork, we collected vast amounts of detailed data on specific work practices that we then sought to interpret. The literature on complex adaptive systems was helpful in this task in three ways. First, this literature is premised on the assumption that details matter—many small actions combine in complex ways to constitute a system. Certainly, we observed many small details that seemed to fit together in ways that represented internally coherent but fundamentally different ways to run a factory. Second, in trying to understand how these detailed work practices all fit together we were drawn to two concepts in the complex adaptive systems literature. We want to be cautious in how we use these concepts, but here is what we found helpful. The literature points out that systems evolve and change through a process whereby "credit" is assigned to actions that parties find constructive. In time, if the credit seems well placed, it becomes a body of information from which system "rules" are codified.

Thus, we saw workers and managers from America and Japan all assigning credit to new patterns, which became manifest in new rules for work. The third lesson from the complex adaptive literature is the particular application of the concept of rules and credit around the issue of kaizen. We began to see the accumulation of small incremental improvements in work processes as an important end in itself as well as part of a larger process of system change. Essentially, kaizen works when people at all levels of an organization are able to channel group wisdom toward incremental improvements and then assign credit based on this learning.

Ultimately, it is in assigning credit and crafting rules that systems are able to adapt to new circumstances. Across our sites, this process is far from complete. On some technical issues, such as running a factory with JIT delivery from suppliers, that adaptation is relatively advanced in most of our sites. On other matters—especially social system issues such as the role of unions in these work settings—we are still in very early stages of assigning credit without any clear rules having yet emerged. As a result, individuals are acting from a mix of old and new perspectives in ways that create confusion and conflict. The ideas on credit and rules are more completely explained in John H. Holland, *Hidden Order* (Reading, Mass.: Addison-Wesley, 1995), 53–80. For more information on complexity and complex adaptive systems, see Ilya Prigogine and Isabelle Stengers, *Order out of Chaos* (New York: Bantam Books, 1984); M. Mitchell Waldrop, *Complexity: The Emerging Science at the Edge of Order and Chaos* (New York: Simon and Schuster, 1992); Stuart A. Kaufman, *The Origins of Order: Self-Organization and Selection in Evolution* (New York: Oxford University Press, 1993).

25. We are indebted to Betty Barrett of our research team for coining this term.

26. Note that such benchmarking is not limited by industrial sector, and the concept has now diffused quite broadly in North American organizations.

27. Masaaki Imai, *Kaizen: The Key to Japan's Competitive Success* (New York: McGraw-Hill, 1984).

28. This has become a well-known concept through its discussion by authors such as Peter Drucker in *Post-Capitalist Society*, and Richard Florida and Martin Kenney, "Transplanted Organizations: The Transfer of Japanese Industrial Organization to the U.S." *American Sociological Review* 56 (1991): 381–398.

29. The Toyota Guiding Principles were taken from company materials.

30. Stephen Hawking, *A Brief History of Time* (New York: Bantam Books, 1988).

31. Daniel Katz and Robert Kahn, *The Social Psychology of Organizations* (New York: Wiley, 1966).

32. When this book was submitted to our publishers, W. Mark Fruin's book, *Knowledge Works: Managing Intellectual Capital at Toshiba* (New York: Oxford University Press, 1997) came to our attention. His book provides a highly focused window into these same dynamics.

Chapter 2

1. In *Toyota Production System: Beyond Large-Scale Production* (Cambridge, Mass.: Productivity Press, 1988), Taiichi Ohno recommends using this method to help truly resolve problems.

2. During the model launch in 1991–92 the line was expanded to three models.

3. We were told to wear our jeans when we returned for the second day of observation and research.

4. We have been told that associates don't wear hats any longer. The Japanese wanted the associates to wear hats, but the Americans didn't want to wear them.

5. Another of our sites, the Coil Center, supplies "blanks" of flat, rolled steel from which some of these parts are stamped.

6. This has changed since our last visit, according to a contact person in Ogihara. There is now a fence around the plant and two security gates. Parking for officers has been assigned.

7. Within this single large building there are actually two separate operations—I/NTek and I/N Kote. The steel from the rolling mill, I/NTek, is

treated by the coating process at I/N Kote. When we were visiting in 1992, the galvanizing section was in the early phase of startup. In this book, we focus on the more established I/NTek organization.

8. Ohno discusses the five S's in his book, *Toyota Production System*. The authors of the present book have also studied how the ideas and concepts of the five S's have diffused beyond the sites in this study to other U.S. companies. It is intriguing to observe the diversity in application and meaning across a sample of facilities.

Chapter 3

1. For example, the 1936 Toyota Model AA passenger car was very similar to the 1934 Chevrolet and had parts compatibility. The parts were available because GM was making Chevrolets in its Osaka, Japan plant. Total Guide to Toyota Commemorative Museum of Industry and Technology, Nagoya, S.T.C. Inc., 1995, p. 90.

2. For an in-depth scholarly description of this transfer process, see D. Eleanor Westney, *Imitation and Innovation: The Transfer of Western Organizational Patterns to Meiji Japan* (Cambridge, Mass.: Harvard University Press, 1987).

3. Co-evolution is defined by Webster as a biological term that means "evolution involving successive changes in two or more ecologically interdependent species (as of a plant and its pollinators) that affect their interactions." We have applied this definition to the organizations and processes we observed.

4. Postwar conditions in both the United States and Japan shaped the development of the industrial base through availability of resources, market preferences, and innovative influences such as the work of Deming and consumer uses of miniaturization. The lessons learned from the Korean War aided in the further development of industrial effectiveness. Japanese industries were exceptionally responsive to information from overseas, which led to creative responses to supply-side demand.

5. Among the works that discuss these issues, see Richard Florida and Martin Kenney, *Beyond Mass Production: The Japanese System and Its Transfer to the U.S.* (New York: Oxford University Press, 1993); T. Abo, ed., *Hybrid Factory: The Japanese Production System in the United States* (New York: Oxford University Press, 1994); James C. Abegglen and George Stalk Jr., *Kaisha: The Japanese Corporation* (New York: Basic Books, 1985); Robert E. Cole, *Work, Mobility, and Participation: A Comparative Study of American and Japanese Industry* (Berkeley: University of California Press, 1979); M. Aoki and R. Dore, eds., *The Japanese Firm: Sources of Competitive Strength* (Oxford: Oxford University Press, 1994).

6. See Jeremiah J. Sullivan, *Invasion of the Salarymen: The Japanese Business Presence in America* (Westport, Conn.: Praeger, 1992).

7. See the epilogue by Mira Wilkins in Abo, ed., *Hybrid Factory*, 257–283, for a thorough explanation of Japanese investment.

8. Among the influential scholars of the transfer of Japanese production systems to the United States was Yasuhiro Monden, who cited a number of

reasons for caution in his book *Toyota Management System: Linking the Seven Key Functional Areas*, trans. Bruce Talbot (Portland, Ore.: Productivity Press, 1993). He pointed out differences between Japanese and North American cultures and production systems—differences that made it difficult for Western workers to fully understand and accept Japanese production methods. Monden (200) also cited the UAW as an important and potential "stumbling block" to part of this process.

9. Although it was not one of our original sites, we visited the Honda facilities in Marysville, Ohio. This site also fits into this category. We are most grateful to Toshikato Amino for insights into the Honda experiences.

10. Davis Jenkins, "Explaining the Transfer to the U.S. of Innovations in Shop Floor Work Systems by Japanese Transplant Manufacturers," working paper, Heinz School of Public Policy and Management, Carnegie Mellon University, 1994.

11. Richard Florida and Martin Kenney, "Transplanted Organizations: The Transfer of Japanese Industrial Organizations to the U.S.," *American Sociological Review* 56 (1991): 381–398.

12. In fact, conversations with Greg Bamber from Australia's Griffith University in Queensland point to a similar pattern with two waves of Japanese investment in Australia—the first of which featured plants that adopted local work practices and the second of which involved the adaptation of Japanese production methods.

13. See Everett Rogers, *Diffusion of Innovation*, 3d ed. (New York: Free Press, 1983), 10.

14. In Abo, ed., *Hybrid Factory*, Tetsuo Abo and others discuss a model they term the adoption and application model, which resembles what we have labeled as imposed.

15. See Michael Indergaard, *The Social and Political Consequences of Industrial Restructuring in Detroit's Downriver Communities.* Ph.D. thesis (Michigan State University, 1990).

16. See chapter 7 for more training and other human resource management issues.

17. Takashi, Inaba, Betty Barrett, Wen-Jeng Lin, and Arthur Wheaton, "Developments in Cross-Cultural Procedural Justice, Industrial Relations, and Human Resource Management," in *The Emerging Issues of Employment*, for the Third Asian Regional Congress of the International Industrial Relations Research Association, Democratization, Globalization, and the Transformation of Industrial Relations in Asian Countries held Sept. 30 to Oct. 4, 1996 in Taipei, Taiwan, R.O.C.

18. See Nancy J. Adler, *International Dimensions of Organizational Behavior*, 3d ed. (Cincinnati: South-Western College Publishing, 1997), 192.

19. Due to the multicultural nature of our research group, we often recognize patterns that occur in our relations. In the area of negotiations, we have often seen a greater concern for the ongoing relationship displayed by Japanese colleagues.

20. David A. Lax and James K. Sebenius, *The Manager as Negotiator* (New York: Free Press, 1986), 30–33.

21. Ikujiro Nonaka and Hirotaka Takeuchi refer to a similar concept when they describe the foundation to their hypertext organization structure in *The Knowledge-Creating Company: How Japanese Companies Create the Dynamics of Innovation* (New York: Oxford University Press, 1995), 166–177.

22. Edward C. Stewart and Milton J. Bennett, *American Cultural Patterns* (Yarmouth, Me.: Intercultural Press, 1991), 16.

23. See James F. Heddinger and Stanley D. Tooley, *Small Town: Giant Corporation* (Lanham, Md.: University Press of America, 1994).

24. In the preface to Michael Harris Bond, *Beyond the Chinese Face* (Hong Kong: Oxford University Press, 1991), p. xx, André Maurois is quoted: "A people is a mirror in which each traveller contemplates his own image."

25. See Everett Rogers and Lawrence Kincaid, *Communication Networks: Toward a New Paradigm for Research* (New York: Free Press, 1981).

Chapter 4

1. Paul Osterman, "How Common Is Workplace Transformation and Who Adopts It?" *Industrial and Labor Relations Review* 47 (1994): 173–188.

2. The Work Practices Diffusion Team first reported on its findings in an article, "Team-Based Work System: Explaining the Diversity," *California Management Review* 37(1994): 42–64.

3. Interviews included shop-floor workers, supervisors, engineers, plant managers, and senior executives.

4. For a vivid description of a visual factory, see Kiyoshi Suzaki, *The New Shop Floor Management: Empowering People for Continuous Improvement* (New York: Free Press, 1993), 213–217.

5. Under this keiretsu system, there is not only common-stock ownership and common ties to investment banks, but there are also high levels of information sharing and joint engineering activities aimed at mutual prosperity.

6. See Janice A. Klein, "A Reexamination of Autonomy in Light of New Manufacturing Practices," *Human Relations* 44 (1991): 21–39; Janice A. Klein, "The Human Costs of Manufacturing Reform," *Harvard Business Review* 67, no. 2 (March–April 1989): 60–65.

7. See Joan Woodward, *Industrial Organization: Theory and Practice*, 2d ed. (Oxford: Oxford University Press, 1980).

8. See, for example, James P. Womack, Daniel T. Jones, and Daniel Roos, *The Machine That Changed the World* (New York: Macmillan, 1990).

9. Examples of this literature include T. D. Rankin, *New Forms of Work Organization: The Challenge for North American Unions* (Toronto: University of Toronto Press, 1990); C. H. P. Pava, *Managing New Office Technology: An Organizational Strategy* (New York: Free Press, 1983); Saul Rubinstein, Michael Bennett, and Thomas Kochan, "The Saturn Partnership: Co-Management and the Reinvention of the Local Union," in *IRRA Annual Research*

Volume (Madison: Industrial Relations Research Association, 1993); Eric Trist, *The Evolution of Socio-Technical Theory* (Toronto: Quality of Working Life Center, 1981).

10. This is similar to Woodward's findings linking organizational structure to production technology (see Woodward, *Industrial Organization*, 2d ed.).

11. Womack and colleagues discuss this in *The Machine That Changed the World.*

Chapter 5

1. Gary Hamel and C. K. Prahalad, *Competing for the Future: Breakthrough Strategies for Seizing Control of Your Industry and Creating the Markets of Tomorrow* (Boston: Harvard Business School Press, 1994), 164–65.

2. It is interesting to note that General Douglas MacArthur and W. Edwards Deming both worked in Japan to change quality and productivity standards. MacArthur was interested in improvements in using radio broadcasts to upgrade the public education system. His appointee, Homer Sarasohn, recommended Deming to give a seminar in statistical process control in Japan. See Michael Pecht and William Boulton, *Japanese Technology Evaluation Center Panel Report on Electronic Manufacturing and Packaging in Japan*, Chapter 6, "Quality Assurance and Reliability in the Japanese Electronics Industry," February 1995, at http://itri.loyola.edu/welcome.htm.

3. Douglas M. McGregor, *The Human Side of Enterprise* (New York: McGraw-Hill, 1960); George C. Homans, *The Human Group* (New York: Bruce Harcourt, 1950); Elton Mayo, *The Human Problems of an Industrial Civilization* (New York: Macmillan, 1933); Frederick J. Roethlisberger and W. J. Dickson, *Management and the Worker* (Cambridge: Harvard University Press, 1939).

4. Theories such as those proposed by Douglas McGregor in *The Human Side of Enterprise* (New York: McGraw-Hill, 1960) or outlined by Frederick Herzberg in *Work and the Nature of Man* (New York: World, 1966).

5. See Barry Bluestone and Irving Bluestone, *Negotiating the Future: A Labor Perspective on American Business* (New York: Basic Books, 1992):

> As early as 1967, delegates to the United Auto Workers collective-bargaining convention approved a resolution that dealt with the basic objective of humanizing the workplace and affording employees a greater measure of respect, dignity, and participation on the job. As chief administrative assistant to Walter Reuther, the union's president, Irving Bluestone wrote that resolution. In part, it read:
>
> > The work place is not a penal colony; it must be stripped of its air of coercion and compulsion; imaginative new ways must be found to enable workers to participate democratically in decisions affecting that nature of their work. There is no reason why human and democratic innovation must continue to lag behind technological innovation in the plants and offices. (*Proceedings of the Special Collective Bargaining Convention* [Detroit, Mich.: UAW, 1967], p. 118.)

When the UAW first brought what it called the "quality of worklife" issue to the bargaining table at General Motors, the company scoffed at the idea. But by 1973, GM agreed to begin implementation of the union-proposed, jointly sponsored "Quality of Worklife Improvement" program, which became known as QWL.

6. See Eric Trist and K. W. Bamforth, "Some Social and Psychological Consequences of the Longwall Method of Coal-Getting," *Human Resources* 4 (1951): 6–24 and 37–38.

7. Taiichi Ohno, *Toyota Production System* (Cambridge, Mass.: Productivity Press, 1988). Original Japanese edition: *Toyota seisan hoshiki* (Tokyo: Diamond, Inc., 1978).

8. Masaaki Imai, *Kaizen: The Key to Japan's Competitive Success* (New York: McGraw-Hill, 1986), xx. Emphasis added.

9. There is a ten-year gap from the time Ohno wrote his book until it was translated into English (see n. 7). This creates a knowledge gap that is difficult to bridge.

10. In Yasuhiro Monden, *The Toyota Management System: Linking the Seven Key Functional Areas*, trans. Bruce Talbot (Portland, Ore: Productivity Press, 1993).

11. Field notes from interview at Hitachi Magnetics on May 1, 1992.

12. An ironic feature of many QWL and QC efforts is that they sought to address individual worker alienation through a group structure that was also capable of increasing rather than reducing alienation as a result of the system barriers constraining the groups.

13. This team structure was being reviewed and we believe it has changed. Team size has been reduced.

14. People are also able to learn about their co-workers through the small personal touches (such as pictures of children), social activities, and humorous elements that appear in these areas.

15. In *Hidden Order: How Adaptation Builds Complexity* (Reading, Mass.: Helix Books, Addison-Wesley, 1995), 53–56, John Holland describes a process by which the assignment of credit "strengthens rules that belong to chains of action terminating in rewards."

16. Wen-Jeng Lin, *Identifying the Determinants of a Kaizen-Suggestion System and Assessing Its Impact on Plant-Level Productivity: A Pooled Cross-Sectional and Time Series Analysis*, Ph.D. thesis (Michigan State University, 1995).

17. Denso representatives who helped review the early versions of this book were quick to point out that workers are considered associates rather than employees.

18. Excerpt from the preamble to the constitution of the International Union, United Automobile, Aerospace and Agricultural Implement Workers of America (UAW).

19. Systems views are described in James P. Womack, Daniel T. Jones, and Daniel Roos's *The Machine That Changed the World* (New York: Macmillan, 1990); Peter Senge's *The Fifth Discipline* (New York: Currency Doubleday,

1990); and W. Edward Deming's *Out of the Crisis* (Cambridge, Mass.: Massachusetts Institute of Technology, Center of Advanced Engineering Study, 1986).

Chapter 6

1. This chapter is adapted from a paper presented at a forum sponsored by the Work in America Institute and the Japan Institute of Labor; Joel Cutcher-Gershenfeld and the Work Practices Diffusion Team (M. Nitta, B. Barrett, N. Belhedi, J. Bullard, C. Coutchie, T. Inaba, I. Ishino, S. Lee, W.-J. Lin, W. Mothersell, S. Rabine, S. Ramanand, M. Strolle, and A. Wheaton), "Constructing Employment Security: Understanding the Emergence of Mutual Commitment," in *Employment Security: Changing Characteristics in U.S. and Japan*, vol. 2 (Scarsdale, N.Y.: Work in America, Inc., 1995), 23–37.

2. Lifetime employment was widely accepted by both management and labor in part because the concept successfully captured the sense of an implied exchange or social contract between employees, who would not resign from company management unless it seriously mistrusted them, and a firm which would not fire workers unless they committed a serious malpractice or faced a real threat to its survival. See Keisuke Nakamura and Michio Nitta, "Developments in Industrial Relations and Human Resource Practices in Japan," in *Employment Relations in a Changing World Economy*, ed. Richard Locke, Thomas Kochan, and Michael Piore (Cambridge, Mass.: MIT Press, 1995), 325–358.

3. Motohiro Morishima, "Japanese Employees' Attitudes toward Changes in Traditional Employment Practices," *Industrial Relations* 31 (1992): 433–454.

4. See Nakamura and Nitta, "Developments in Industrial Relations and Human Resource Practices in Japan."

5. Note that traditional workplaces operating this way are not just unionized settings. Civil service procedures set up similar structures, and many nonunion service and manufacturing operations rely on seniority preference even in the absence of a union.

6. Among recent items are Louis Uchitelle, "More Downsized Workers Are Returning as Rentals," *New York Times*, Dec. 8, 1996, Sec. 1, p. 1; Keith Hammonds, "The Issue Is Employment, not Employability," *Business Week*, June 10, 1996, p. 64; Donald McNerney, "The Cost of Loyalty Lost" (interview with Frederick F. Reichhard), *HR Focus*, June 1996, p. 18; Jeremy Rifkin, "A New Social Contract," *Annals of the American Academy of Political and Social Science* 544 (March 1996): 16.

7. For more detail on the start of this American phenomenon, see Michael Hammer and James Champy's *Re-engineering the Corporation: A Manifesto for Business Revolution* (New York: Harper Business, 1993).

8. We use this as it is described in Robert Ozaki's book, *Human Capitalism: The Japanese Enterprise System as World Model* (New York: Penguin, 1991).

9. See chapter 5.

10. Richard Walton, Joel Cutcher-Gershenfeld, and Robert McKersie, *Strategic Negotiations: A Theory of Change in Labor Relations* (Boston: Harvard Business School Press, 1994).

11. 1994 contract between the United Auto Workers and Auto Alliance Inc., Article 7, p. 12.

12. It should be noted that many unionized Japanese-affiliated operations do not have contract language on employment security. This reflects, in part, the difficulty in making such guarantees for smaller, second- and third-tier suppliers. For example, the same UAW local that represents the workers at AAI also represents workers at three other Japanese facilities, but these organizations have all resisted union pressure to sign language on employment security.

13. This provision raised serious concerns at the time of our visits since there were worries that Inland might lay off up to 25% of its workforce.

14. Note that the management resources face a fundamental employment security challenge in this system given the ambiguity that then arises over just what value they add.

15. There have been some problems since then. According to the UAW website (UAW.ORG), there was a strike over retiree health benefits and a pension freeze.

16. See Kenichi Ohmae, *The Borderless World: Power and Strategy in the Interlinked Economy* (New York: Harper Business, 1990).

17. A good illustration of this philosophy is outlined in Ozaki, *Human Capitalism*.

18. See Ikujiro Nonaka and Hirotaka Takeuchi's *The Knowledge-Creating Company: How Japanese Companies Create the Dynamics of Innovation* (New York: Oxford University Press, 1995). The authors discuss their concept of a hypertext organization, which is founded on an organizationally developed and shared base of knowledge.

19. See Nakamura and Nitta, "Developments in Industrial Relations and Human Resource Practices in Japan," in *Employment Relations in a Changing World Economy*, 325–358.

20. John Zhuang Yang, "The Rationale of Maintaining Job Security—A Study of Japanese-Owned Plants in the U.S." (paper presented at the Association of Japanese Business Studies Meetings in New York, N.Y., 1993), 2.

21. As of 1997, there were well over 600 employees at Ogihara.

22. Their situation is comparable to the middle managers who are increasingly less central to work group operations.

Chapter 7

1. As Taiichi Ohno points out in *Toyota Production System: Beyond Large-Scale Production* (Cambridge, Mass.: Productivity Press, 1988), the development of these principles in Japan did not spread until the middle to late 1970s, when these practices proved more valuable in surviving the two major oil crises during that decade. Subsequently, the processes have continued to evolve, and there is still great variation today in Japan.

2. Note that many of these practices are also found in the United States, though the meaning and details are fundamentally different since they are not

embedded in a context that is focused on the long-term building of capability of the workers in an employment security context.

3. See chapter 6 for more discussion of social contracts.

4. George T. Milkovich and Jerry M. Newman, *Compensation* (Chicago: Irwin, 1995), 300.

5. Functional silos of expertise combine with Tayloristic assumptions to create an unintended consequence that robs knowledge from individual tasks.

6. Among auto assembly and supply firms, there is frequently a desire to remain union free. Locating in rural areas does not guarantee that the firms will remain union free. In fact, some unions are targeting the supply plant as an organizing strategy—see the discussion of the UAW local at AAI in chapter 8. Richard Florida and Martin Kenney reinforce the idea that the relationship rather than the location determines unionization in *Beyond Mass Production: The Japanese System and Its Transfer to the U.S.* (New York: Oxford University Press, 1993), 101–103.

7. Authors such as Joseph and Suzy Fucini describe primarily negative race relations between the Japanese and blacks at the Mazda plant in Flat Rock in their book *Working for the Japanese: Inside Mazda's American Auto Plant* (New York: Free Press, 1990), 116–118. Ruth Milkman also comments on relations with minorities and women in *Japan's California Factories* (Los Angeles: Institute of Industrial Relations, University of California, 1991), 7–8. Milkman feels that the situation in Japanese plants in California does not reflect the nationwide view.

8. Fierce competition between locales for a factory often found regions rather than states or communities bidding for the presence of a factory that could provide jobs and economic development to an area. See Robert Perrucci, *Japanese Auto Transplants in the Heartland: Corporatism and Community,* Social Institutions and Social Change series (New York: Aldine de Gruyter, 1994).

9. Ernie Lofton was the UAW region 1A director during the early days of the Flat Rock plant. He appointed Bill Judson as the first president of UAW Local 3000. One accounting of the role of these union officials at the Mazda Flat Rock plant is found in Fucini and Fucini, *Working for the Japanese.*

10. See Edward E. Lawler, *High-Involvement Management* (San Francisco: Jossey-Bass, 1986).

11. Each site has different ways of handling pay and compensation for their employees. This may be further complicated by multiple sources of salary within a site. For example, an employee might be paid by the U.S. site while the next employee might be paid by the headquarters in Japan.

12. See Nonaka's discussion of middle-up-down management of knowledge creation.

13. Ikujiro Nonaka and Hirotaka Takeuchi, *The Knowledge-Creating Company: How Japanese Companies Create the Dynamics of Innovation* (New York: Oxford University Press, 1995), 84, talks about the process of socialization as one way of viewing interpersonal communication in a workplace. Other authors discuss the importance of interaction between workers in the creation

of a functional knowledge base that serves the individuals as they serve the firm. See Julian E. Orr, *Talking about Machines: An Ethnography of a Modern Job* (Ithaca, N.Y.: Cornell University Press, 1995); Jean Lave, *Cognition in Practice* (Cambridge: Cambridge University Press, 1988); Robert E. Cole, *Strategies for Learning: Small-Group Activities in American, Japanese, and Swedish Industry* (Berkeley: University of California Press, 1989).

14. Nonaka and Takeuchi, *Knowledge-Creating Company*.

15. For one comparison of knowledge and information, see ibid., 57–59.

16. See chapter 8 for an in-depth discussion of complementary and symmetrical relationships.

Chapter 8

1. See George Taylor, *Government Regulation of Industrial Relations* (New York: Prentice-Hall, 1948), and Thomas A. Kochan, *Collective Bargaining and Industrial Relations* (Homewood, Il: Richard D. Irwin, 1980).

2. See Thomas A. Kochan, Harry C. Katz, and Robert B. McKersie, *The Transformation of American Industrial Relations* (New York: Basic Books, 1986).

3. See chapter 3 for a discussion of the implications of the timing of Japanese investment.

4. See James P. Womack, Daniel T. Jones, and Daniel Roos, *The Machine That Changed the World* (New York: Macmillan, 1990), 252.

5. Much as in the process of normal science described by Thomas S. Kuhn, *The Structure of Scientific Revolutions* (Chicago: University of Chicago Press, 1962), 24.

6. For example, GM pursued its so-called southern strategy by building plants in Alabama, Louisiana, Texas, and Oklahoma in the 1960s.

7. See Richard E. Walton and Gerald L. Sussman, "People Policies for the New Machines," *Harvard Business Review* 65 (1987): 98–107.

8. See chapter 7 for further discussion of human resource management issues.

9. Some managers might say these words, but it is truly rare for a manager to operate in a system where the words can be matched by actions.

10. See the startup at NUMMI in which the UAW felt compelled to report health and safety concerns to CALOSHA to get relief.

11. Our research focused on I/NTek. However, there is an interesting relationship between I/N Kote and I/NTek. They are independent companies in the same building, with a management and union leadership structure that covers both firms. The roller quality problems occurred at I/N Kote.

12. Kochan, Katz, and McKersie, *Transformation of American Industrial Relations*.

13. "Symmetrical" and "complementary," terms borrowed from anthropologist Gregory Bateson, describe aspects of the variation in U.S. labor relations. See Gregory Bateson, *Naven* (Stanford: Stanford University Press, 1958),

176–177. Bateson used the term "symmetrical" to describe relations between contending male members of a tribe, where interactions involved parallel, culturally validated, mutually reinforcing competition. He used the term "complementary" to describe relations among family members where the interactions were complex, interdependent, and oriented around constructing bonds. We are drawn to these terms since they describe relationships rather than structural circumstances (which is the case for the term "enterprise," for example).

14. Inaba, Takashi, Betty Barrett, Wen-Jeng Lin, and Arthur Wheaton, "Developments in Cross-Cultural Procedural Justice, Industrial Relations, and Human Resource Management," in *The Emerging Issues of Employment*, eds. S. C. C. Kang, Y. Huang, and L. Lin (Taipei: Association of Industrial Relations, R.O.C., 1996), 143–164.

15. Joseph Fucini and Suzy Fucini, *Working for the Japanese: Inside Mazda's American Auto Plant* (New York: Free Press, 1990), 149, 183; Mike Parker and Jane Slaughter, *Choosing Sides: Unions and the Team Concept* (Boston: South End Press, 1988).

16. Henry Ford, quoted in Henry Ford and Samuel Growther, *Today and Tomorrow* (New York: Doubleday, 1926), 160, as cited in Barry Bluestone and Irving Bluestone, *Negotiating for the Future: A Labor Perspective on American Business* (New York: Basic Books, 1992).

17. Terry A. Beehr, Jeffrey T. Walsh, and Thomas D. Taber, "Relationship of Stress to Individually and Organizationally Valued States: Higher Order Needs as a Moderator," *Journal of Applied Psychology*, 61 (1976): 41–47.

18. Lindsey Chapell, "It's NUMMI Forever or NUMMI No More," *Automotive News*, July 5, 1993, p. 16; Tsukasa Furukawa and Al Wrigley, "Toyota, GM to Extend Venture; New Agreement Would Continue NUMMI Indefinitely," *American Metal Market*, July 5, 1993, p. 7.

Chapter 9

1. Collaborative work is of great interest today. It is a fundamental part of techniques such as scenario planning and group software applications. Among the books that discuss these techniques is Peter Schwartz, *The Art of the Long View* (New York: Doubleday, 1991); a more in-depth companion book is Kees van der Heijden, *Scenarios: The Art of Strategic Conversation* (Chichester, England: John Wiley and Sons Ltd., 1996). Michael Schrage talks about creative collaboration in *No More Teams!: Mastering the Dynamics of Creative Collaboration* (New York: Doubleday, 1990); a case can be made that management techniques can be a form of collaboration such as those discussed in John Case, *Open-Book Management: The Coming Business Revolution* (New York: Harper Collins, 1995).

2. For further discussion, see Henry Mintzberg, *The Structuring of Organizations: A Synthesis of the Research* (Englewood Cliffs, N.J.: Prentice-Hall, 1979).

3. Among the current works on the idea of assessing the values of intangible factors are Thomas A. Stewart, *Intellectual Capital* (New York: Doubleday,

1997), and Karl E. Sveiby, *The New Organizational Wealth* (New York: Berritt-Koehler, 1997).

4. See Bertram H. Raven, "The Bases of Power: Origins and Recent Developments," *Journal of Social Issues* 49 (1993): 227–252. This article is a revision of a 1959 work by Raven and French on the bases of power.

5. Toshikata Amino from Honda emphasized the importance of people not just finding meaning in work but supporting what he called the joy of work. A part of his responsibilities at Honda involved inspecting potential suppliers. He told us that he would always make it a point during a site inspection to use the bathroom farthest from the executive suite in a factory. If this was neat and clean, that was an indication that people had pride in their work and workplace—both of which were prerequisites for workers to appreciate the joy of work.

Index

Edmore, Michigan, Hitachi Magnetics plant in, 22–23, 40, 76

Employee Assistance Program (EAP), 29

Employee involvement groups/ teams, 62, 64

Employee involvement and kaizen, 71–72

employee involvement driving knowledge creation within boundaries, 78–80

employee involvement targeted at reducing waste, 80–83

historical context, 72–76, 171n.2

implications for employee power in knowledge-driven work systems, 83–85

knowledge creation without employee involvement, 76–78, 172n.12

Employment security, 88–90

additional risks for organizations and institutions, 106–107

defining employment security in practice, 90–97

in Japan, 10–11

labor relations and, 142, 148

linking employment security to the production system, 97–103

practices in unionized and nonunionized sites, 92–97

who is at risk?, 103–106

England, STS model in, 133

Enterprise labor relations, 130, 138, 139, 149

Enterprise unionism, 131, 144

Explicit knowledge, 4, 5, 57, 123, 157

Exploitation of workers, 131

Federal Mediation and Conciliation Service, 77

Federal Trade Commission (FTC), 147

First-line supervisors, 104, 105

First-wave of Japanese investment in the United States, 39–40

First-wave sites/firms

employment security at, 91, 92, 93

human resource management practices at, 112, 119–120

Five S's, Japanese, 34–35, 55

Florida, Richard, 41

Flow-through manufacturing, 86

Ford, Henry, 141

Ford Motor Company, 50, 62, 73, 120

Fremont, California, NUMMI plant in, 13

Fucini, Joseph and Suzy, 141

Gagnon, Mike, 96–97

Gainsburger Pet Foods, 73

Gender discrimination, racial and, 111, 175n.7

General Electric (GE), 40, 45

General Motors (GM)

compensation issues at, 120

Fremont plant, 55, 98, 114

GM–Toyota joint venture, 147

NUMMI and, 13, 43, 52, 56, 62

QWL at, 73

Saturn operations, 133, 161

Global diffusion of work practices, 4, 160–162, 163n.3

capital investment and, 9

industrial relations and, 8

knowledge-creation process in, 5

Grand Rapids, Michigan, Yamaha Musical Products plant in, 23–25

Greenfield and brownfield sites, 20, 138

Greetings, 54

Hamel, Gary, 72

Heddinger, James, 52

Printed in the United States
83111LV00003B/67-81/A

9 780195 114546